P9-CEW-634

GROVE PRESS MODERN DRAMATISTS

Grove Press Modern Dramatists
Series Editors: *Bruce King* and *Adele King*

Published titles

Further titles in preparation

GROVE PRESS MODERN DRAMATISTS

FEMINIST THEATRE

An Introduction to Plays of Contemporary British and American Women

Helene Keyssar

Grove Press, Inc., New York

First published in 1984 by
Higher and Further Education Division
MACMILLAN PUBLISHERS LTD
London and Basingstoke

First Grove Press Edition 1985
First Printing 1985
ISBN: 0-394-54631-8
Library of Congress Catalog Card No. 85-70226

First Evergreen Edition 1985
First Printing 1985
ISBN: 0-394-62059-3
Library of Congress Catalog Card No.85-70226

Manufactured in the United States of America

GROVE PRESS, INC.
196 West Houston Street, New York, N.Y. 10014

1   3   5   4   2

Contents

List of Plates

7. John Boswall as Mr Emanuelli and Jane Carr as Mary Mooney in *Once a Catholic* by Mary O'Malley, at the Royal Court Theatre, 1977. © Donald Cooper.

8. *Crimes of the Heart* by Beth Henley; Lee Anne Fahey, Kathy Bates, Susan Kingsley, at the Actors Theatre of Louisville, 1979. © David S. Talbott.

9. *Skirmishes* by Catherine Hayes at the Hampstead Theatre, 1982; Gwen Taylor as Rita, Anna Wing as Mother and Frances de la Tour as Jean. © Donald Cooper.

10. The New York Festival Production for Public Theatre in October 1976 of *for colored girls* ... by Ntozake Shange. © Martha Swope.

11. Susan Kingsley and Lynn Cohen in *Getting Out* by Marsha Norman, Actors Theatre of Louisville, 1977. © David S. Talbott.

12. Ian McKellen as Colin and Gemma Jones as Anne in *Ashes* by David Rudkin, Young Vic, 1975. © Donald Cooper.

Every effort has been made to trace all the copyright-holders, but if any have been inadvertently overlooked the publishers will be pleased to make the necessary arrangement at the first opportunity.

ANNE: But Susan B. why do you not say these things out loud.

SUSAN B.: Why not, because if I did they would not listen they not alone would not listen they would revenge themselves. Men have kind hearts when they are not afraid but they are afraid afraid afraid. I say they are afraid, but if I were to tell them so their kindness would turn to hate. . . .

Gertrude Stein, *The Mother of Us All*

Editors' Preface

The *Macmillan Modern Dramatists* is an international series of introductions to major and significant nineteenth- and twentieth-century dramatists, movements and new forms of drama in Europe, Great Britain, America and new nations such as Nigeria and Trinidad. Besides new studies of great and influential dramatists of the past, the series includes volumes on contemporary authors, recent trends in the theatre and on many dramatists, such as writers of farce, who have created theatre 'classics' while being neglected by literary criticism. The volumes in the series devoted to individual dramatists include a biography, a survey of the plays, and detailed analysis of the most significant plays, along with discussion, where relevant, of the political, social, historical and theatrical context. The authors of the volumes, who are involved with theatre as playwrights, directors, actors, teachers and critics, are concerned with the plays as theatre and discuss such matters as performance, character interpretation and staging, along with themes and contexts.

BRUCE KING
ADELE KING

ix

To my mother Grace and her sisters
Jane, Gertrude and Florence
and to my own sister Redwing

Preface: Transformations

Theatre has always attracted me because of its inability to lie about its own authenticity. Even the most casual spectator knows when a performance is 'set', presented from rote to get through the evening, and when it is alive, ready to meet and change with the audience. The challenge in writing books, and, for me, this book in particular, was to capture that sense of discovery, of surprise in a medium whose very nature is characterised by permanence and finitude.

Writing about feminist drama has made that task ironically easy. When I began this project, I thought that I had a fairly good sense of the terrain and its divisions. The essential characteristics of feminist drama seemed to be the creation of significant stage roles for women, a concern with gender roles in society, exploration of the texture of women's worlds and an urge towards the politicisation of sexuality. I had a hypothesis that within the frame of these shared concerns was a significant conflict about the most effective form for feminist plays. Some playwrights claimed that feminist drama was in the process of returning theatre to a more truthful mode of realism whereas others urged that the genre was liberating theatre from the restrictive conventions and middle-class biases of realism. I took this to represent contrasting commitments to an exploration of the psychology of women on the one hand and the social and political status of women on the other, and I associated the first position with American playwrights and the second with British playwrights.

None of this turned out to be entirely wrong, but nor was it as simple or accurate as I originally imagined. There are few plays discussed in this book that do not diverge significantly from conventional realism, not because of a bias in my selection but because of the persistent inclinations of feminist dramatists. All of the plays discussed, however, attempt to capture genuine and often disregarded details of women's lives; they strive for authenticity but often the 'reality' that is their goal is not a matter of a photographic surface image but of a metaphor that captures the elusive rather than the manifest gesture. In fact, I have learned from this study to be suspect of the implications of the term 'realism'. While the label certainly helps us to gather a group of plays ranging from Henrik Ibsen's *A Doll's House* to Marsha Norman's *'night, Mother*, it does not follow that plays in an obviously different mode, plays that, for example, defy chronology or ordinary language usage, are by definition 'non-realistic'.

I would now argue, then, that the tension I initially perceived is not a matter of conflict between realistic and non-realistic dramaturgies but a matter of different angles and proximities of points of view. Perhaps because the desert paintings of Georgia O'Keefe – landscapes all – strike me as a good backdrop for almost every feminist play I know of, I would liken the differing perspectives found in feminist drama to different approaches to the desert. From a distance, in certain lights, and especially in the summer and winter, the desert appears drab, mute and single-hued. But the closer one gets, and particularly in the spring, one finds not only variations of tone and sound but at times such intensity of colour and melody that it is difficult to draw away. Both visions of the desert are equally true and 'real', just as the feminist drama that presents a female character wearing the mask of a rat's head is as 'real' as one in which a woman lifts her skirt and appears to urinate on stage.

That the presence or absence of realism is not *the* central issue for feminist drama does not mean that all these plays are alike or that there is no pattern to feminist dramaturgy. Divisions remain between emphases on interiority as opposed to exteriority, between works that separate and works that conjoin class consciousness and gender consciousness, between plays that focus on women's autonomy and those that stress community. In England, many feminist playwrights are also socialists, deeply concerned with class and its relation to gender, with production and its relation to reproduction. Few American feminist playwrights would call themselves socialists, and many more American feminists take a psychological approach to their work.

More important than these distinctions, however, is the relentless appearance in these plays of the strategy of transformation, the theatrical manifestation of metamorphosis of contexts, actions and, most crucially, of characters. In contrast to most of the drama of the last two thousand years, feminist drama does not rely on a recognition scene as the pivot of its structure.

In his key perception about Greek tragedy, Aristotle argued that drama achieved its effect on the audience by presenting a character who comes to know himself (or herself), and whose moment of self-recognition is revealed to others. Drama has thus traditionally urged us to know ourselves better, to search our histories and to *reveal* to ourselves and others who we 'really' are. In feminist drama, however, the impetus is not towards self-recognition and revelation of a 'true' self but towards recognition of others and a concomitant transformation of the self and the world. The female characters who are at the centre of feminist drama change in front of our eyes, sometimes gradually and sometimes suddenly. In most pre-feminist dramas, protagonists strip away their disguises and defences, leaving us to see and acknowledge the true Clytemnestra or the true Nora. Traditional heroism lies in this process of recognition and unveiling. Even in psychoanalytically oriented feminist plays, however, the self is not seen as stable and hidden but as shifting, alterable, admirably and problematically varied. Nor is the world in which characters exist reassuringly unified and solid, but fragmented and diverse.

This emphasis on transformations enriches and clarifies the feminist slogan 'the personal is political'. Drama that pivots on recognition scenes, where the goal is to stand still and 'know thyself' is essentially conservative; it seeks and embraces what *is* and confirms the power of individual consciousness. Drama that embraces transformations inspires and asserts the possibility for change; roles and role-playing, not hidden essences, merit attention; we are what we do and what we become, and no one, neither woman nor man, is restricted from becoming other.

I am not certain, in the end, that this turn towards transformations is ultimately best realised in the live theatre. A striking number of feminist dramatists exploit cinematic conventions in their plays, and when film learns from the hesitant example of theatre and becomes more accessible to feminist perspectives, it may well turn out to be the more fertile medium for feminist production.

I am certain, however, that the plays I discuss in the following pages all merit more extensive production and acknowledgement than they have thus far received. Drama anthologies and textbooks continue to collect almost exclusively plays by and about men. And while feminist perspectives gradually influence commercial theatre, drama schools and departments in universities continue to teach and produce the traditional repertoire with little sense that the women who will work in the theatre of the future, and many of the men as well, are seeking not just new roles but different kinds of roles and ways of playing.

This book describes the alternatives proposed by feminist drama and the resources that exist and wait to be read, seen and performed. Early on I made a decision, not entirely happily, to focus my attention on plays that have been published, are likely to be published, or are readily available because of their continuing production histories. Many of the plays described in these pages were developed in collaboration; on the other hand, most collaborations are not published or reproduced on the assumption that they are less commercially viable than those with the stamp of one person's authority. Other critics and historians of the theatre – Honor Moore, Michelene Wandor, Karen Malpede to name just a few – focus more on the terrain of unpublished works by collectives and one-of-a-kind endeavours, and I urge readers to turn to their studies for different glimpses of the landscape.

My study of feminist drama has changed not only my thinking about the genre but my consciousness of myself and the world around me. A number of books and essays never directly mentioned in these pages have contributed significantly to what I say about the plays themselves. A brief list of those that inform these pages would include the works of Nancy Choderow, Dorothy Dinerstein, Juliet Mitchell, Carol Gilligan, Julia Kristeva, Hélène Cixous, Luce Iragaray, Sheila Rowbotham and Catherine A. MacKinnon. Another kind of context that frames this book is the University of California Feminist Theater and Video Ensemble, whose diverse and generous members gave new life to some of these plays. Equally generous in their support of my work have been members of the Communication Department staff: I thank C. Jane Geddes who gave particular help at key moments and I especially thank Lynn Lindsey and Jillaine Smith, who worked patiently and with wonderful efficiency on the preparation of the final typescript. Jillaine Smith was a member of the first UCSD Feminist Theater Ensemble and knew just how and why this manuscript mattered. The Regents of the University of California supported my research with a grant that enabled me to interview playwrights, see productions and gather material in the United States and England. Bruce and Adele King, the series editors, prodded me long distance in just the right ways and did a fine and fast job of editing at the end of this enterprise; I especially appreciate their rigorous reading of Chapter 8. Finally, there is my own less public context, repeatedly enriched and transformed by Tracy B. Strong, Catherine Portuges and Carol Axel, each of whom has shared with me the experience of renewal that feminist drama can bring.

HELENE KEYSSAR
San Diego

1
Roots and Contexts

Feminist drama emerged as a distinct theatrical genre in the late 1960s in both Britain and the United States. Although plays about women have existed since the origins of drama, and plays by women have been written and performed in the Western world at least since Sappho, it was not until the last decade that playwrights in significant numbers became self-consciously concerned about the presence – or absence – of women as women on stage. Parented by the women's movement and the 'new theatre', feminist drama had its most immediate roots in the political and aesthetic disruptions of the 1960s. As the contemporary playwright Honor Moore has remarked, whether or not they identify themselves publicly and politically as 'feminists', there are now playwrights whose 'art is related to their condition as women'.[1] The plays created in the context of that recognition do not just mirror social change but assert a new aesthetic based on the transformation rather than the recognition of persons.

Gertrude Stein, whose operas and scores for the theatre

1

in the first half of the century were among the first overtly feminist dramas, described her plays as 'landscapes'. Her works were indeed terrains for playing, not slices of reality but segments or visions of the world crammed with nuance, with shadow and light, and deliberately left fluid for performance. The concept of a play as a landscape, while de-emphasising the plot, usefully embodies the importance of texture and detail in feminist drama. Important, too, to the notion of feminist drama as landscapes is the diffusion of the playwright's attention among a number of characters. 'After all,' Stein remarked, 'to me one human being is as important as another human being, and you might say that the landscape has the same values, a blade of grass has the same value as a tree.'[2] In contrast to much Western drama, characters in feminist plays only rarely transcend their contexts; more frequently, they grapple with and attempt to reorder the ordinary activities of everyday life. Feminist playwrights often behave like explorers, sending back maps for their audiences of apparent but uncharted territories. The lands and cities they reveal are not remote or exotic; they are the places of women, and they have been there all along. Only now, however, they are being discovered and illuminated.

The characters who inhabit these landscapes are usually but not exclusively women. A number of the most effective plays in the genre do banish men from the stage world; in Ntozake Shange's *for colored girls who have considered suicide when the rainbow is enuf* or Pam Gems's *Dusa, Fish, Stas and Vi* men are only present in references in the women's conversations and the absence of men on stage itself becomes a forceful gesture. But the absence of men as well as the particular roles created for men in feminist plays are rarely simple matters of revenge or rectification. To the surprise of many spectators, few feminist dramas are primarily assaults on men. More frequently, feminist plays attempt to pay attention to the lives of women – as individuals, in relation to each other, and in relation to men.

This often takes the form, closely associated with other aspects of the women's movement, of re-presenting women who played important but forgotten roles in history or of retelling history from a female perspective. Plays like Viveca Lanfors's *I Am Woman* and Eve Merriam's *Out of Our Father's House* use the stage both to inform the audience of the deeds and struggles of women who altered history and to sound the cry of women's voices, to break the silence too often characteristic of women's place in drama. More recently, some of the most powerful feminist dramas have captured moments in history from strikingly distinctive angles of vision: Caryl Churchill's *Vinegar Tom* and *Cloud Nine* and Wendy Kesselman's *My Sister in this House*, for example, present perspectives on history that emphasise women's social roles as defined by their sexuality. In re-presenting history, these plays call into question conventional notions and theatrical expressions of sexuality and relationships of power to gender.

While not all feminist dramas are overtly concerned with power and politics, taken together these plays present an overwhelming argument for the inseparability of sexuality and gender from politics. Equally important, many of these plays exploit the very nature of theatre to demonstrate the distinction between gender and sexuality. It is not in biologically defined sexual identity but in social gender roles that power is allocated and enacted on stage. In the theatre, the actor is able to take on *any* identity or character role. Audiences for ancient Greek drama, for the Elizabethan theatre, for classic Chinese opera, not only accepted the playing of female characters by men, but assumed the actor's ability to take on many roles, both male and female. Transformations of gender and the variability of roles in contexts have thus always been implicit components of theatre. Plays like Eve Merriam's *The Club*, Caryl Churchill's *Cloud Nine* and Megan Terry's *Hothouse*, pay attention to this inherent possibility of theatre by requiring the performance of male characters by women and female characters by men and by only partially disguising these transformations. Other feminist dramas, like Myrna Lamb's *But What Have You Done for Me Lately?* or Megan Terry's *Comings and Goings* create worlds in which men engage in traditionally 'female' activities. Such gestures free the stage for a fuller, more complex exploration of erotic and social behaviour among all human beings and make gender transformations political.

The relationship of theatre to audience always conjoins and juxtaposes private life and public life, but except in Greek tragedy where the chorus rendered the private public, the spectator has been the unseen voyeur of the character's most private moments. And even in Greek drama, the stance of the playwright was to be distant or invisible. In contrast, a significant number of feminist playwrights and performers have consciously drawn on their own lives for the stories and characters that structure their plays, and, rather than attempting to disguise this autobiographical tendency, have proclaimed it as an important assertion of presence. In the past, when women have been allowed to speak or appear in public it has been *in disguise*, hidden behind make-up, veils, deceptive clothing, carefully regulated movement, names that obliterate their own identities or make them tangential to a man. It is therefore appropriate that one radical gesture of feminist theatre is to decrease the distance between playwright and actress, actress and character, to build without distortion or protection the stories told on stage from the experiences of those who make theatre. Theatrical and personal vulnerability are thus asserted rather than hidden. In a frequently cited statement of this tenet, the New York feminist theatre company, It's All Right to Be Woman articulated this approach:

> We make theatre out of our lives, our dreams, our feelings, our fantasies. We make theatre by letting out the different parts of us that we have pushed inside all our lives. . . . Making theatre out of these private parts of ourselves is one way we are trying every day to take our own experiences seriously, to accept our feelings as valid and real.[3]

The obvious danger in this emphasis on the personal, confessional resources of feminist drama is that it becomes too idiosyncratic or simply too constrained by the particular life experiences of a few playwrights. One way feminist drama tries to avoid this obstacle is by collective scripting of various kinds. Feminist theatre companies in both Britain and the United States have often created their own scripts for performance, and, rather than assigning the task of playwriting to one member, they have frequently arrived at scripts through the collaboration of everyone involved. In Britain during the seventies and early eighties, the Women's Theatre Group, Red Ladder Theatre, Gay Sweatshop, Joint Stock, and Monstrous Regiment each produced collectively devised feminist productions. Beginning somewhat earlier, in the late sixties, the Rhode Island Feminist Theatre, It's All Right to Be a Woman, Circle of the Witch, the New Feminist Theatre, the New York Feminist Theatre Troupe, Caravan Theatre, the Alive and

Trucking Theatre Company, the Omaha Magic Theatre and at least a dozen other women's theatre groups performed collectively created works in the United States. Most of these companies followed a similar process: out of discussions of their own life-experiences, the group would arrive at a theme or set of related motifs – mother–daughter relationships, abortion and work were among those frequently pursued – and then a smaller group would work out a structure for the show. After further discussion, the company would spend considerable time in games and improvisations to explore theatrically the stories they had shared; relatively late in the process, specific roles would be taken on and a script would be recorded.[4] This mode of scripting often results in what Honor Moore has called 'choral plays', dramas that focus on groups of women rather than on one female protagonist. By presenting a variety of equal voices, these plays structurally avoid enclosure in one point of view.

Such full-scale collective scripting continues, but other modes of collaboration have tended to replace the company script. The reasons are varied. Many of these scripts are contextually bound to parochial issues and individual histories; they are exhaustive of time, money and energy. In addition, there is still sufficient resistance to any kind of collective work that neither producers nor publishers are eager to support plays that cannot be identified with a 'unique' individual. The notion prevails that originality is an individual attribute and is tainted by dialogue with others.

In response to these obstacles, some companies have simply modified the concept of the script subcommittee such that responsibility for scripting shifts from one member to another or is taken on by one or two participants who are particularly skilled as playwrights. More frequently, women engaged in playwriting will be commissioned by a theatre or company to work with the players and director to develop a script. Pam Gems, Michelene Wandor and Caryl Churchill have all worked in this way in Britain, as have Susan Miller, Megan Terry and Myrna Lamb among others in the United States. Still other playwrights like Ntozake Shange and Paula Moss, Eve Merriam, Paula Wagner and Jack Hoffsiss, Margaretta D'Arcy and John Arden have created their scripts jointly with other writers.

Still another, more severe attempt to minimise the coercion of written words has appeared in the creation of deliberately skeletal or flexible scripts that necessitate or allow a second stage of writing. Texts like Susan Miller's *Cross Country* or Viveca Lanfors's *I Am Woman* provide sufficient structure and language for a company to begin work while leaving many specific dramaturgical and performance decisions to each particular troupe. The playwrights present the material on the page in ways that urge the performers to renegotiate, to cut and add. On the page, Miller's work looks like a collage of prose and dialogue; the actors and director must give dramatic form to *Cross Country*. Lanfors's play allows for roles to be performed by any number of participants and provides for the easy substitution of speeches, voices and characters. Like other modes of collaboration these, too, are part of the feminist resistance to hierarchy and authoritarian control.

These efforts have not, of course, sprung whole from the new feminism of the last two decades but are rooted in the ensemble concept initially articulated around 1830 by the Russian writer Gogol and his associate, the actor Shchepkin. Gogol and Shchepkin urged theatrical production to rid itself of its adulation of stars and instead aim for the subordination of individual performances to the overall effect of the performed drama. Stanislavsky was much

influenced by the directions taken by Gogol and Shchepkin, and, in his own work with the Moscow Art Theatre,
made the ensemble a *sine qua non* of good rehearsal
process: 'What is important to me,' he wrote, 'is that the
collective creation of all the artists of the stage be whole
and complete and that all those who helped to make the
performance might serve for the sake of the same creative goal and bring their creations to one common
denominator.'[5]

It is possible to argue that the realisation of that dictum
became the driving force behind every significant theatre
performance since the turn of the century. But although
Stanislavsky included 'all the artists of the stage' in his
concept of 'collective creation', he did not confront the fact
that as long as men and women remained unequal in society
and in the scripts that reflected the social world, authentic
collectivity was impossible.

It was not until the 1950s when a resurgence of
experimentation in the theatre brought renewed energy to
the ensemble concept, that concern with the structure of
theatrical production began to make conscious links to
women's roles. In Britain, Joan Littlewood directed and
inspired the Theatre Workshop which produced both
innovative revivals of classical works and new plays, of
which the most notable were those of Brendan Behan and
Shelagh Delaney. The Theatre Workshop combined a
commitment to social change with serious attempts to
organise its own procedures in a collective fashion;
Littlewood herself persistently objected to the acclaim she
received for the success of the company's productions on
the grounds that the strength of the Workshop's productions lay in the 'hard-won ability of its actors to work
self-effacingly as a team'.[6]

Ironically, one of the aspects of the Workshop that was

most disconcerting to reviewers was its acknowledged involvement in the shaping of new scripts. Utilising a method that was to become central to companies in the sixties and crucial to the emergence of feminist drama, the Workshop actors improvised from scripted materials, and these improvisations in turn transformed the script. With curiosity and some suspicion, critics and audiences perceived these rehearsal procedures and the choice of plays as 'female-dominated'.

In 1956, another new company, the English Stage Society, made its first appearance at the Royal Court Theatre, under the director George Devine. Committed to the production of new plays and open to work that called attention to class consciousness, the English Stage Society at the Royal Court sought to transform the British theatre from the museum showcase it had become by the mid-fifties into an innovative and socially influential activity. Yet, in its search for new playwrights, the only woman it 'discovered' was Ann Jellicoe, and although the plays it produced were concerned with socially 'relevant' topics, few of them presented any significant challenge to the class or gender structure of the worlds they portrayed.

During this period, the seeds of the 'new theatre' in the United States were planted by Judith Malina and Julian Beck, founders in 1946 of the Living Theatre. Malina's and Beck's first concern was to create a theatre supportive of poetic drama, a theatre that encouraged poets to write plays and that rejected the living-room realism of most mainstream theatre. Over the next twenty years, including periods of significant economic and ideological disruption, the Living Theatre brought new and unproduced dramas to the stage and was a centre for experimentation in theatrical styles. In the early fifties, it was one of the few companies to produce the plays of Gertrude Stein.

Feminist Theatre

From the womb of the Living Theatre sprang the American experimental theatre of the sixties. Joseph Chaikin, originally an actor with the Living Theatre, founded the Open Theatre in 1963 to seek new theatrical forms and new rehearsal techniques. Writers and directors, among them Megan Terry and Roberta Sklar, were included in the extensive games and exercises developed by the Open Theatre from Viola Spolin's theatre games and Jerzy Grotowski's work with the Polish Laboratory Theatre. As the Open Theatre developed, it increasingly stressed 'sound-and-movement' exercises that co-ordinated physical and oral gestures independent of semantic or representational content. The Performance Group, the Manhattan Project, the Theater of the Ridicul-ous, and other new companies like the Caravan Theatre in Boston and the San Francisco Mime Troupe followed similar but distinguishable paths to that of the Open Theatre, most-often creating scores that necessitated improvisation in performance as well as in the rehearsal process.

Much of this experimentation, particularly when it meant the production of new scripts by unknown play-wrights or collaborations, was nourished by one extraordi-nary woman, Ellen Stewart, who, in 1961 established her Café La Mama in a basement in the East Village of New York City. Stewart's focus, like that of the English Stage Society, was on the discovery of new drama; more relent-lessly than any other theatre artist of the time, she searched for plays that had little resemblance to living-room dramas.

Improvisation, process, environment, transformation and audience-relationship were the keywords of these companies and theatres, all of which saw themselves in rebellion against what Peter Brook proclaimed as the 'dead theatre' of Broadway, the West End and the like. As the names of many of these companies, including the Theatre Workshop, suggest, the goal was a theatre that exploded the barrier between art and life. Performances were viewed in a continuum with rehearsals, the stage as an isolated platform was abandoned, actors took on multiple roles, often transforming identity from one character to another in full view of the audience. The use of transformations as a technique and concept whereby actions, objects and characters were fluidly altered from one identity to another soon revealed a device that could be exploited to explore sex-based roles.

It was in this 'new theatre' in the United States that lines purposefully began to be blurred between the actor as a person with a life-history outside the theatre and the actor-as-character: towards the end of the Open Theatre's *Mutation Show*, one of the women in the company, Ellen Maddow, introduced herself and her co-performers to the audience, announcing not only their 'real' names but providing genealogies and bits of descriptions that remarked something of each performer's context outside the theatre. The personal was half-consciously becoming political.

Feminist drama is indebted to these experiments yet none of them significantly altered the domination of contemporary drama by men and by an imbedded masculine vision of the world. One hindrance to change was the cult of personality that inspired and bound most of the new theatre companies. Despite the important presences of Joan Littlewood, Roberta Sklar, and Ellen Stewart, and in part because of the attempts of these women to undermine their own roles as charismatic leaders, most of the new theatre experiments were dominated by and identified with particular men. George Devine, Michel Saint-Denis, Peter Cheeseman, Peter Brook, Peter Hall, Joseph Chaikin,

Richard Schechner and Andre Gregory were the names that emerged in the public sphere as the leaders of the new theatre of the sixties. And with Samuel Beckett, Harold Pinter and Edward Albee leading the way, it was again male playwrights who led the published lists of the major new playwrights of the era. Ann Jellicoe, Shelagh Delaney, Lorraine Hansberry, Adrienne Kennedy, Rochelle Owens, Maria Irene Fornes, Megan Terry and Rosalyn Drexler all wrote award-winning plays during the late fifties and sixties, but while drama courses and anthologies quickly absorbed the new male playwrights, their female counterparts remained obscure.

The 'new' theatre simultaneously revealed and barricaded the way for women in theatre. At the same time, the political movements of the sixties, especially in the United States, were unknowingly running a parallel course. Beginning in the early sixties, significant numbers of American women, most of them young and middle class, forsook the shelter of suburban domesticity and threw their energies into the civil rights movement, the student movement and the anti-war movement. They taught in freedom schools, ran voter registration projects, set up libraries, rode buses across the South; in disproportionate numbers, these women stuffed envelopes and kept the offices of the Student Non-violent Coordinating Committee (SNCC), the Committee on Racial Equality (CORE), the Southern Christian Leadership Committee (SCLC), and the Students for a Democratic Society (SDS) running – and clean. On freedom rides and marches, they were threatened, assaulted and not infrequently arrested and jailed. Women in these movements embraced the 'new left' emphasis on community and challenged bourgeois family structure along with racism, poverty, imperialism and nuclear armament. They supported the anti-bureaucratic, non-hierarchical structures that were to keep the people involved in the movement. In particular, many American women, early on, saw in the model of black power an opportunity to challenge and change sexual inequality in their personal and social lives. Armed with Betty Friedan's *The Feminine Mystique* (1962), the pill and a new self-confidence gained through political work, women began to question their own investments in sexual monogamy, economic dependency and public impotence.

The parallels between the activities and ideals of American new theatre artists and new left workers are striking. Both movements placed high value on collective activity, striving for an authentic sense of community within the group as well as a deep engagement with the audience or community they served. The notion borrowed from Jerzy Grotowski of a 'poor theatre', a theatre stripped of ornament and focused on the elemental and transcendent possibilities of the actor, had its equivalent in the new left emphasis on action – on sit-ins and door-to-door registration – and in the evolving counter-cultural lifestyle. Both movements challenged the authority and authorities of established institutions; although Americans in the sixties rarely voiced their concerns in terms of class conflict or class consciousness, poverty became an issue inseparable from racism, the elitism of academic institutions and the war in Vietnam. Underlying both the new theatre and the new politics was an impassioned rejection of complacency and a somewhat romantic vision of personal and social transformation: taking risks became good in itself and to be vulnerable was paradoxically to be strong.

For many women involved in the American political movements the romance was short lived. By 1965, a number of women, particularly white women involved in the civil rights movement, were beginning to rebel against their own relative powerlessness. Discrepancies between the rhetoric of political equality and practice when it came to women had taken its toll. In a paper indicting gender-based discrimination in SNCC, Casey Hayden and Mary Varela claimed that although women kept the movement running on a day-to-day basis, they had little say in policy decisions.[7] Other women were noting that almost all of the position papers put out by movement organisations appeared under the names of men, even when women had contributed significantly to their authorship. Equally disturbing to many women was the exploitation of their attempts to rethink personal relationships in the context of movement politics. Remarks like Stokely Carmichael's notorious 'The only position for women in SNCC is prone', infuriated women and brought their confusion about sexual behaviour to the fore. In political gatherings as well as in theatre companies, sexual diversity became a sign of liberation, but for many women freedom from the constraints of traditional sexual mores quickly became an objectifying dogma.

Between 1965 and 1968, the growing self-consciousness of American women outside as well as within the 'movement' appeared in the public sphere. In 1965, a group of professional women, many of whom had been involved in state commissions on the status of women, founded the National Organisation of Women (NOW); their initial aim was to lobby for the civil and economic rights of women in education, work and media representation. As student protests and anti-war activities accelerated in 1966 and 1967, women began to protest against male definitions of work and the abstract, impersonal style of movement rhetoric. By late 1967 women's liberation groups had formed in Chicago, New York, Boston and Toronto. The forerunners of consciousness-raising circles, most of these

14

early women's groups were formed spontaneously by women who found themselves in long conversations about their roots and frustrations in civil rights or student movement organisations. Within a year, thousands of women were meeting in small groups all over the United States. Their goal was to raise each other's consciousness of the plight of women by sharing stories of oppression and private struggle for autonomy and self-confidence. These were, as they came to be called, support groups, gatherings of women who had wished to support each other's struggle for self-respect.

Once the women's movement erupted in the United States, it was only a matter of months before its resonances were heard in Britain and before women in the theatre in both countries recognised the potential for a new feminist theatre. In the absence of a coherent civil rights movement and in the presence of a significantly more structured and overtly socialist left-wing movement, women in England were a step behind American women in both articulating their distinct concerns and forming into separate groups to confront feminist issues. Yet legislation that affected women was and has remained more progressive in Britain than in the United States: while sixties civil rights laws cleared some paths for women in the United States, the legality of abortion was left to the courts, reforms in divorce laws occurred slowly at the state level, and the Equal Rights Amendment was defeated in 1982. In contrast, in Britain both an Abortion Act and an act partially legalising male homosexuality were passed in 1967, a Divorce Reform Act was passed in 1969 and the Equal Pay Act of 1970 set the legal path for a gradual rectification of women's economic status.

For women in both countries the key to a distinct women's movement was in the acceptance of the notion that 'the personal is political'. The challenge in that slogan was significantly different for American women than for their British sisters. For Americans, most of the sixties was spent in becoming politically conscious, in recognising that women could indeed take on political roles. Because the politics in which American women in the sixties were nurtured had ostensibly stressed the fusion of personal and political life, once American women accepted and desired political roles, there was no difficulty in acknowledging that 'the personal is political'; that, in turn, meant that politics had to deal with gender. But while it was relatively easy by the late sixties for American women to place their psychological struggles in the context of politics, it was and is still difficult for Americans to consider class conflict as central to politics and to their particular concerns as women. For women in Britain, however, the framework of politics was class structure, and at least one obstacle in the women's movement was a clear understanding of the relationship between gender conflict and class conflict.

Significant numbers of women in Britain had been active on the 'New Left' and/or members of the Communist Party, the Committee for Nuclear Disarmament (CND), the Labour Party Young Socialists, the International Socialism Group (IS), tenants' associations, trade unions and community workshops. Rather than gradually becoming politicised, these women had struggled through internal disputes on the left that focused on the necessary confrontation with Stalinism after 1956. While American women who barely knew the name Leon Trotsky were desegregating restaurants and public transportation, British women were running free schools and community workshops but were also arguing the relevance of Lenin's doctrines to the problems of inequality in Britain in the sixties. The American women who moved from civil rights work into

16

the student movement or the anti-war movement tended to be white women who found their racial identity (especially when coupled with their sexual identity) to be an increasing obstacle to useful work. In Britain, however, many women moved from one 'New Left' group to another because of changes in their conscious political perceptions: some women switched from local community-oriented groups to national or international party organisations, and others moved in the opposite direction out of a similar desire to have more impact on social change. Unknown to each other, however, women in both countries were struggling with common issues: the failure of political groups to reorganise their own structures so as to undermine a psychology of leadership, the resistance of most groups to genuine consideration of the political meanings of the ways people lived their ordinary lives, and the persistent subordination of women to men.

It is still difficult to sort out the interrelationships of the political and cultural explosions that occurred world-wide in 1968. What is clear is that students, in some instances with workers, dramatised their dissatisfaction not just with governments but with the fabric of daily life. The public demonstrations of 1968 were undeniably theatrical, made more so perhaps by the ability of television and radio to transmit dramatic visual images to a vast public. In the United States particularly, theatre and politics were haunting bedfellows as millions of spectators witnessed assassinations as well as strikes and protest marches on their television sets. When, in the autumn of 1968, a number of women's groups produced a theatrical protest using street-theatre conventions against the sexism of the Miss America pageant, it was an event coherent with the collusion of theatre and politics in other corners of society. It was also, however, the first instance in which the resurgent women's movement had achieved significant public acknowledgement. Two years later, women in Britain would protest against the Miss World event in a similar theatrical demonstration. Feminist theatre had been born.

It now needed to discover and rediscover the scripts that would make it endure, and that endeavour faced two immediate obstacles. The first was obvious: as Virginia Woolf had made poignantly clear forty years before in *A Room of One's Own*, the social structure in which theatre has existed for more than 2000 years made it unlikely that a 'Judith Shakespeare', talented as we might imagine her, would achieve recognition as a playwright. And, although a number of women playwrights had seen their works published and produced in the twentieth century, even in the late 1960s the networks of money and power that brought drama to the public remained not only primarily controlled by men but intimidatingly impenetrable for most women.

Equally important, even once the women's movement and feminist theatre had begun to assert their presence, many feminist playwrights deliberately resisted definition of the genre. Particularly in its early stages, some practitioners felt that to define the genre was to place inappropriate constraints on a form that aimed at diversification. To avoid the simple replacement of one elite and compound voice with another, it was argued that no individual voice should bear the *authority* of definition. It was not that this voice was necessarily wrong or corrupt, unimaginative or even unrepresentative of the group as a whole, but that it carried power that no other individual or group as a whole could equal. The Polish Laboratory Theatre was defined by Grotowski; Peter Brook articulated the goals of theatrical innovation in England; despite the recognised contributions of prominent colleagues, Joseph Chaikin spoke for

18

the Open Theatre. In order to escape this domination and the hierarchical structure it implied, a number of women left established theatre companies, including ones that were self-consciously experimental or political. In 1972, when Charlotte Rea was researching an article on women's theatre groups for *The Drama Review*, she found that in order to report on one group's activities, she had to meet with everyone who was available and that 'when it became necessary to have the material checked for accuracy, the whole group was consulted'.[8] Michelene Wandor's research on feminist theatre groups in Britain revealed a similar commitment, as was directly stated by the Women's Theatre Group: 'our group, as a byproduct of the Women's Movement, has already functioned in a totally collective manner, trying to avoid leadership and hierarchies'.[9]

A second reason that playwrights resist or disclaim definitions of feminist drama is their hesitancy to be associated with feminism as a social and political movement. Some deny the existence of a distinct feminine sensibility and claim that when they focus on women, or reveal gender as a political and social issue, they are simply expressing their individual, idiosyncratic perspectives. They refuse to associate their endeavours with a group, a genre or an ideology. Still others argue that feminist drama's association with the women's movement makes it susceptible to charges of didacticism; just as for some, any gathering named feminist or emphasising women is automatically seen as lesbian and therefore either man-hating or sexually 'perverse', so theatre overtly associated with women is sometimes facilely reduced to demonstrations of hostility towards men and towards heterosexuality.

Despite these resistances, since the early sixties approximately 300 plays by women have been published in Britain and the United States; more than half of these arise

out of an acknowledged and apparent feminist consciousness, and many others are illuminating of women's roles
and their relationships to men in society. At least another
100 feminist plays have been produced but remain unpublished. Published and unpublished feminist plays have won
recognition in both Britain and the United States. In 1981
alone, Caryl Churchill's *Cloud Nine*, Beth Henley's *Crimes
of the Heart* and Wendy Kesselman's *My Sister in this
House* won major prizes. The public emergence of a genre
of feminist theatre has also begun to ease the way for
publication of collections of feminist plays such as those
edited by Michelene Wandor in Britain and Honor Moore
in the United States. The publication in 1981 of two very
different but equally serious studies of feminist consciousness in the theatre, Wandor's *Understudies*, and Helen
Chinoy and Linda Jenkins's *Women in American Theatre*,
marks yet another recognition that feminist theatre is no
longer a tenuous experiment.

As important as these indices of public acknowledgement, is the vitality of a complex network of artists and
audiences committed to feminism in the theatre. Among
the first signs of such a network was the formation in New
York in 1972 of the Women's Theater Council, a group of
six women playwrights dedicated to the discovery and
production of new plays by women. Each of the founding
members – Maria Irene Fornes, Rosalyn Drexler, Julie
Bovasso, Adrienne Kennedy, Rochelle Owens and Megan
Terry – had written a number of produced plays, but all
were in agreement that the mainstream New York theatre
was insufficiently supportive of plays by women. Their aim
for their first season was to produce in repertory one play
by each of the founding members, but their larger vision
was of a 'mighty corpuscle' that served as a magnet to other
plays by women. The plays they produced would escape the

reductions these women perceived in the 'masculine-oriented theatre'; gone would be the 'bitch, the goddess and the whore with the heart of gold'. 'Men are writing out of their dreams', Irene Fornes told Mel Gussow, the *New York Times* critic, on the occasion of the formation of the group. 'Ours are feminine dreams. Now we can say yes, we are women.'

A year after its creation, the Women's Theater Council evolved into Theater Strategy, a larger group of twenty-three playwrights that now included male playwrights like Ed Bullins, Sam Shepard and John Ford Noonan. Although that group, too, gradually dissolved its formal ties, in part because of insufficient funding, many of the women involved have continued to make special efforts to encourage and support each other's work and work by new women playwrights.

In Britain, the first network of feminist dramatists was comprised of a series of threads drawn from socialist groups, agit-prop theatre, lunch-time theatre and an experimentally inclined group concerned with theatre in education. In 1973, Ed Berman, an American by birth, and founder of the Almost Free Theatre, organised a lunch-time festival specifically of plays by women; meetings to read scripts and plan the festival were open to any woman who wanted to attend, and the response was substantial.

During the early seventies, the Arts Council in England was moderately supportive of new 'fringe' theatre groups, but in 1975, it cut much of this funding. In response, thirty playwrights formed the Theatre Writers' Group, and a year later, they and others formed the Theatre Writers' Union. The majority of members were men, but both male and female feminist playwrights were influential in the organisation. These groups and the informal network sustained by Michelene Wandor have brought a feminist perspective to a variety of productions.

2
Foothills:
Precursors of
Feminist Drama

The roots of feminist drama wind through the history of the
theatre, but their adequate uncovering remains the task of
research only now being conducted. Both the feminist
theatre movement and feminist drama were foreshadowed
in the hundreds of plays by women written in the early part
of the twentieth century and more recently in a dozen
powerful works by women dramatists in the 1950s and
early 1960s. Current research calls attention to the
seventeenth-century plays of Aphra Behn, and comedies
and melodramas by women playwrights such as Cora
Mowatt in the nineteenth century. These were not only
plays *by* women but plays that pointedly revealed the
complexities of women's lives and that subverted assumed
notions of women's social powerlessness.

These are relics, of course, and of all such evidence
perhaps the most astonishing is the plays of Hrosvita, a
tenth-century sister of the 'free' Benedictine Abbey of
Gandersheim. Hrosvita, whose name translates as 'loud
mouth', made no attempt to conceal her identity as a

woman; her plays are prefaced with the comment that while 'it is generally believed that a woman's intelligence is slower', she none the less offers her work to the learned as evidence that she is a 'teachable creature'.

Hrosvita's seven plays, written in rhymed Latin verse, were rediscovered and introduced to European audiences in 1501 by the German poet Conrad Celtes, and in the centuries that followed she was hailed as 'the mother of German wit' and the 'wonder of women'. She merits such praise on at least two counts: first, she remains the only dramatist – male or female – whose works remain intact from a period generally considered to be entirely absent of theatrical scripts. In addition, however, her plays persistently portray the triumph of women over men, and not in the pietistic tone one might expect of a playwright who drew her plots from the legends of the saints. Her dramaturgical model was the Roman playwright Terence, from whom she drew a comic structure that she utilised to challenge male aggression. In Hrosvita's *Dulcitius*, an arrogant Roman governor sets out to rape three virgin Christian sisters, but his lustful fantasies so overwhelm his sanity that he instead embraces the sooty pots and kettles in their kitchen. In one of her most acclaimed plays, *Abraham*, a young woman secretly becomes a prostitute but finally rejects her demeaning occupation and reclaims her soul. Hrosvita's insistence on the positive value of female virginity may be disconcerting to modern women, but her use of laughter as a survival tactic for both her female characters and her plays strikes a remarkably contemporary note.[1]

Over the centuries, a number of women theatre artists have found inspiration in Hrosvita's plays, but few more fruitfully than Christopher St John, a twentieth-century British writer who, in addition to writing eighteen original plays, translated Hrosvita's *Paphnutius* and edited many of the letters and writings of the brilliant actress Ellen Terry. Like many contemporary feminist playwrights, St John's work inside and outside the theatre was overtly political: she was active in the early twentieth-century suffragette movement and helped to found the Writers' Franchise League.

The conjunction of politics and drama in St John's writing is particularly evident in *How the Vote Was Won*, one of the two plays she wrote in collaboration with another early British feminist playwright, Cicely Hamilton. Written in support of the Women's Political and Social Union in Britain, the play was quickly recognised by American suffragettes as an exceptionally seductive vehicle for their movement and was performed repeatedly in the United States, especially on the West Coast. Swiftian in its satiric jabs, *How the Vote Was Won* proposes a moment in history in which women take literally the law's assertion of their dependency on men. Towards the beginning of the play, Horace Cole, 'an English master in his own house' smugly proclaims his opposition to women's right to vote. Within a brief afternoon, however, he is ready to march on parliament for women's rights as he is confronted with an assortment of his female relatives who have all decided to leave their jobs and households and move in with Horace, who, as their nearest male kin, is responsible for taking care of them. The play not only reveals the absurdity of the logical extension of a social configuration in which women are dependent on men but also demonstrates the potential power of women. Horace cannot endure the deluge of the company of women who invade his household, but he is equally oppressed by the social upheaval caused by the women's strike: with no secretaries, maids, seamstresses to sustain daily life, the middle-class men decide to 'escape' to

the theatre, only to discover that with no actresses performing, the theatres, too, are closed. With a strategy identical
to that with which Douglas Turner Ward fifty-five years
later demonstrated the dependency of American whites on
blacks, Hamilton and St John make an indisputable
argument for the male masters' reliance on their female
'slaves'. They also provide a welcome laugh for those who
have quietly known all along that the sky would come
tumbling down the moment they ceased to hold up their
'half'.

Less ostensibly political, but of importance to the
groundings of feminist drama, is the engaging ambience of
the community of women who gradually fill every corner of
the stage in *How the Vote Was Won*. Horace is physically
and dramaturgically squeezed out of the dramatic space of
the play as his house is entered by one woman after
another. The biting wit of the women is sufficiently pleasing
that the audience cannot help but concur with Aunt Lizzie,
who, after ascertaining Horace's absence, declares 'Just as
well, we can talk more freely.'

With the demise of suffragette plays once the vote was
won – in England in 1918 (restricted to those over thirty
until 1928) and in the United States in 1919 – feminist
drama became increasingly rare. Between 1919 and 1960,
the most persistent gesture towards feminism in drama was
a focus on female characters and the particular obstacles
these characters encountered *because* they were women.
Susan Glaspell's *Trifles*, published in 1920 and performed
with increasing frequency in recent years, remains the
provocative archetype of that form. Starting from the
conventionalised frame of the murder-mystery melodrama, Glaspell shifts the object of her point of view from
the male detective and his search for the culprit to two
middle-aged rural women who are left to potter in the

kitchen while the men officiously search for clues that will substantiate indications that it is Minnie Wright who has murdered her husband, John. The strategy of the play rests on building our complicity with the women on stage who gradually uncover the oppression under which Minnie Wright lived with her husband. Because of the kind of details to which the women pay attention, both motivation and narrative clues confirm that Minnie murdered her husband, but, in a quiet act of bonding, the two women suppress what they have learned. By making us acknowledge a woman's world, the play exposes a space usually ignored on-stage, and once we see this inner life, the murder appears justified.

A similar tight and secret women's world appears in a number of plays of the 1920s, many of which have been called 'folk plays' because of their unveiling of the lives of ordinary people for whom the daily challenge is simply to endure. A poignant example of this genre is Georgia Douglas Johnson's *Plumes* in which a black mother and her friend wash and sew in the kitchen of a meagre two-room cottage, while a doctor visits a young daughter who is dying in the next room. The dialogue between the two women is punctuated by their attention to their work and concerns a choice between spending a few hard-saved dollars on an operation for the girl or saving the money for a funeral with 'plumes'. For the two central characters, the choice is not between the momentous and the mundane but is a matter of deciding how to proceed so as to preserve the dignity of both the mother and her daughter. Johnson demands that we enter the black, female culture of her characters and judge their actions *from within that world*. It is a risky attempt but one that is necessary if the audience is genuinely to acknowledge these women within their own context.

The characters in the most-celebrated example of these plays of women's lives, Lillian Hellman's *The Children's Hour*, are also isolated both by and from the presumably normative culture. But whereas both *Trifles* and *Plumes* merit more attention than they have received because they unveil distinctive and complicated value structures that could constructively alter social relations, *The Children's Hour* serves as a negative model of women's theatre and helps to clarify key differences between plays by and about women and feminist drama. Because *The Children's Hour* ostensibly brings lesbianism to the stage – a subject that was and to some extent remains part of a culture of whispers, it appeared to be a radical theatrical event. Its plot, characterisations and form, however, refute its own potential for disruption.

Within moments after the opening curtain of *The Children's Hour*, the audience's attention is riveted on a mean and spiteful young girl who torments both her classmates and her teachers. Frustrated in her attempts to manipulate her teachers (Martha and Karen), the girl, Mary, accuses them of having a lesbian relationship. Public knowledge of this accusation transforms the warm and trusting intimacy of Martha and Karen's friendship into a frightened and forced interdependency between the two women. Public revulsion at the story of the two women's sexual intimacy corrodes their relationship and eventually results in the termination of Karen's engagement to her male lover, Joe, and in Martha's suicide.

The ambiguity of Hellman's strategies in relation to women is ironically and fully present in this, her first play, initially produced in 1934. While the on-stage confrontation with society's unreflecting rejection of lesbian women is in itself a radical act, Hellman's manoeuvres with and around her subject undermine the potential force of her play. On the page and in performance, the strongest emotion evoked from the spectator is that of rage at the spoiled and malevolent girl who initiates the gossip as revenge against her teachers' thwarting of her will. Mendacity and social hypocrisy are the real issues of the play, not friendship or erotic attractions between women.

That in itself does not make *The Children's Hour* an anti-feminist play, but the work goes further to support implicitly society's unhesitant rejection of lesbianism. Our anger at the nasty girl and the community of which she is a part is strengthened and evoked by the persistent revelation of evidence that Karen and Martha are not lovers. We are, then, left, like Karen, with no appropriate response when Martha 'confesses' that she in fact has been erotically attracted to her friend and colleague. Karen's first reaction is to tell Martha that she is crazy, and she insists throughout the confession scene that Martha is ill. If the intentions towards the audience at this point are ambivalent – do we empathise with or reject Karen's response? – Martha's subsequent suicide neatly removes the spectator from any necessity of confronting an actual sexual relationship between two women.

The realism of the play's dramaturgy makes Hellman's confusing strategy particularly troubling. It is not simply that the realistic theatrical mode as used by Hellman is mundane and uninventive, as other critics have commented, but that it suggests that we as audience are seeing an authentic and typical relationship between two women. We are made to be voyeurs in much the same manner that television soap-opera engages its audience, and like such televised drama, what we see is more apt to confirm than challenge assumptions about others based on fear and ignorance. The woman who acknowledges her sexual attraction to another woman is rejected by everyone, including the friend she loves, and is filled with such self-loathing that she kills herself. But the play swiftly suppresses the off-stage violence and concludes by reassuring us that the one 'decent' and normal woman in the play will not only endure but will no longer have to suffer. The last image of the play is of Karen, smiling, in a new sunlight that she tells us 'feels very good'.

The Children's Hour as well as Hellman's later plays confirm stereotypical images of women and establish little affection or respect for female characters. Although the women in Hellman's most commercially successful play, *The Little Foxes* (1939), dominate the stageworld, none of them suggests a constructive or alternative way of being a woman in American culture. Much as Martha's fate and character in *The Children's Hour* confirm the impossibility of being a happy lesbian. Regina, the central character in *The Little Foxes* reifies images of the business woman as a cold and calculating narcissistic creature. A number of lines in the script explain Regina's cruelty and selfishness as a result of inequities brought on by her condition as a woman, but no matter how an actress works with this role, our glimpses of Regina's earlier oppression are obscured by the unyielding self-interest that culminates in her murder of her husband. Her antithesis, Birdie, exemplifies the enslavement of the 'little wife' who is literally treated like a bird-brain; here, too, the play's narrative structure counters the appealing and empathetic eccentricities evident in Birdie by drowning the character in her own drink and removing her from the stage. The only admirable female characters in the play are Addie, the black maid, and Alexandra, Regina's daughter, but Addie's servility is never called into question, and Alexandra is never more than a skeletal extension of her father, the centre of moral vision in this world.

Hellman's more recent work makes even more clear the insufficiency of her dramaturgy within the frame of feminist theatre. *The Autumn Garden*, written and produced in 1951, again presents a man, Crossman, who serves as the *raisonneur*, the voice of wisdom and insight, against a group of women who are victims and fools. One woman in the play, Sophie, is able to take her life in her own hands, after being used by a series of women and men. Yet, despite a near-rape moments before, Sophie's reward for the assertion of her own autonomy is to be accused by another woman of being 'a tough little girl'. That the word here is 'tough' and not strong is a key to the ambivalences that resonate from the stage. It is not only that the men in *The Autumn Garden* are significantly more interesting and independent than the women, but that their cleverness and independence are established as exemplary models. More troubling still, the play presents us with moments of friendship and intimacy between various men, but the women, while denigrated for their dependency on men, are not allowed any stage space in fruitful or comforting contact with each other. Hellman's last play, *Toys in the Attic* (1960) seems only to confirm finally and ironically the desperate dependency of women on men: here, Carrie, motivated by her incestuous love for her brother, attempts to make him dependent on her, but what we see is that she as well as the other women in the play derive their identity from their male-focused passions.

Stylistically, Hellman's craft is inherited by an American female playwright whose work emerged in the fifties, Alice Childress. But Childress's plays, while reliant on the same realistic conventions, move towards a more complex image of women. The first black woman playwright to have her work produced professionally off-Broadway, Childress repeatedly winds the tension of her dramas around a strong and rebellious female character. *Trouble in Mind*, first produced in 1955, is unabashed in its evocation of empathy for its protagonist Wilmetta Mayer. Wilmetta is a middle-aged black actress who is cast in the play-within-the play as an ageing servant for a white Southern family. Grateful at first to have a substantial Broadway role, Wilmetta is increasingly uncomfortable with the play's caricature of blacks and finally turns the white director's demands for 'truth' against the production itself: there is no truth, she declares, in a scene in which a mother – black or white – knowingly sends her son to an unjust death.

While *Trouble in Mind* is most immediately a black social protest play whose context and inspiration is the racial integration movement of the fifties, it is also a play *about* roles in which female stereotypes are acknowledged and jarred. Wilmetta at first behaves humbly before the theatre jargon of some of her better-educated, more sophisticated colleagues, but, in the end, the production in which she is involved so violates her sense of authenticity that she breaks her silence and acquiescence. Judy, the young, white Yale Drama School graduate, is a bundle of liberal clichés, but she relieves the caricature near the end of the play in her recognition of her own posturing and her laughing assertion that 'everyone's a stranger and I'm the strangest of all'. Even Millie, the black lady of the lot who defines herself as a consumate consumer, has a moment of strength when she feels like going out on the street and 'crackin' heads'.

These fleeting glimpses of female strength, mere hints of possibility in *Trouble in Mind*, are enlarged and confirmed fourteen years later in Childress's *Wine in the Wilderness* (1969). Written during the period when feminist drama was just beginning to emerge as a genre, *Wine in the Wilderness* is informed by its attention to black conscious-

ness *and* female consciousness. The protagonist, a thirty-
year-old black factory-worker whose unconventional sexuality is apparent in her name, Tommy, rebels against her
degradation by other blacks whose values are drawn from
the white, middle-class society. Unencumbered by the
professional and class conventions that partially define
Wilmetta in *Trouble in Mind*, Tommy not only fights to
maintain her own dignity but is one of the first genuinely
independent women of the American stage. Too trusting at
first of a pretentious trio who adopt her as the perfect
model of the 'nigger', she learns and teaches that the true
'wine' in the wilderness is not to be judged by her
'accessories' but is a 'woman that's a real one and a good
one'. Tommy longs for romance and the affection and
companionship of a man, but she convinces us and herself
that she is able to make it on her own. Importantly,
however, her realisation of her own autonomy is coupled
with her understanding that talk among her new Afro-
American acquaintances of 'sisters' and 'brothers' is mean-
ingless where there is no genuine 'we-ness'. Tommy
demands a real sense of mutual responsibility and respect.

Tommy is a startlingly assertive leap from Childress's
hesitant Wilmetta of the previous decade. But American
drama in the years between 1955 and 1969 is notably
marked by the emergence of a number of other black
women playwrights who increasingly drew their female
characters with sharp and bold lines. Of these, the plays of
Lorraine Hansberry attracted the most public attention.

Lorraine Hansberry's four plays – *A Raisin in the Sun*,
The Sign in Sidney Brustein's Window, *To Be Young,
Gifted and Black* and *Les Blancs* (the last two of which were
finished after her death by the playwright's husband,
Robert Nemiroff) – are most frequently heralded because
of their poignant protests against racial injustice. Espe-

cially for white audiences, *A Raisin in the Sun* sounded an immutable plea for recognition of the frustrated aspirations of black Americans. In its juxtaposition of white bigotry against the struggles and despair of a warm, witty, black family, *A Raisin in the Sun* became one of the most successful cultural gestures of the integrationist movement. Examined closely, the play's unreconciled contradictions between the family's middle-class values and working-class jobs are disconcerting, but as a theatrical and political event *A Raisin in the Sun* was unquestionably important. Winner of the Drama Critics' Circle Award for best American play of the 1958–9 season, *A Raisin in the Sun* not only played to thousands of spectators for almost two years on Broadway, but also provided new access to the theatre for black artists.

Because the play's focus is the struggle of a man, Walter Lee, to find and sustain his own sense of self-respect, and because of its timely attention to racial inequity, Hansberry's provocative portrayal of women in *A Raisin in the Sun* is often overlooked. The most memorable female character in the play, Mama, is in no way liberated or even questioning of stereotypes of women. But Mama's daughter, Beneatha, and her daughter-in-law, Ruth, are two of the most interesting women to appear in traditional American drama.

Equally important, and more crucial to the development of the genre of feminist drama, Hansberry persistently calls attention to the roles of these women and the ways they are perceived and denigrated by the central male character. The play has hardly begun before Walter Lee starts criticising black women as a group and his wife in particular for their lack of support for black men. Annoyed at Ruth's disinterest in his plans to invest in a liquor store, Walter erupts: 'Man say to his woman, I got me a dream. . . . His woman say, eat your eggs and go to work. Man say, I'm choking to death baby! And his woman say, Your eggs is getting cold.'[2] Within the context of the first scene of the play, the strategy of this speech is to elicit empathy for Walter as opposed to the women who surround him. Even white men can laugh in harmony at the female focus on the mundane. The exchange can also be read as a larger indictment of the black woman's culpability in the socal creation of the impotent black male. Yet it is this same man who shortly reveals his unwillingness to acknowledge Ruth's strength and anguish: the combination of the family's poverty and Walter's narcissism have led Ruth to consider aborting the baby she is carrying, but even this news, conveyed to Walter by Mama, does not distract his focus from his own desires. Throughout the play it is Ruth who continues to work as a domestic in order to support her son, husband, mother-in-law and sister-in-law.

Hansberry's assault on men's attitudes towards women and her belief in women's own perspicacity are even more evident in the scenes that focus on Beneatha, Walter Lee's sister. Beneatha wants more than anything to become a doctor; for her, the money the family is about to inherit is a down-payment on her medical-school tuition. Walter's disdain for these plans and his blatant chauvinism are no secret in this household. Beneatha's entrance is greeted by Walter's pronouncement that she is 'a horrible-looking chick at this hour', and he proceeds from there to demand why she couldn't just be a nurse 'like other women – or just get married and be quiet'. Nor is Walter the only man in this world to make and assert such assumptions about women's roles. One of Beneatha's beaux, an African man named Asagai, refuses to believe that Beneatha wants anything more from her life than a conventional romance with a man. When Beneatha protests that there is more than one kind of feeling possible between a man and a woman, Asagai laughs his denial; when Beneatha then acknowledges his love for her but says it isn't enough, he responds, 'For a woman, it should be enough.' The exchange that follows contains the seeds of the next twenty years of feminist politics and drama:

> BENEATHA: I know – because that's what it says in all the novels that men write. But it isn't. Go ahead and laugh – but I'm not interested in being someone's little episode in America or – [with feminine vengeance] – one of them!
> [Asagai has burst into laughter again]
> That's funny as hell, huh!
> ASAGAI: It's just that every American girl I have known has said that to me. White – black – in this you are all the same. And the same speech, too!
> BENEATHA: [Angrily] Yuk, yuk, yuk!
> ASAGAI: It's how you can be sure that the world's most liberated women are not liberated at all. You all talk about it too much![3]

As a document of both American social history and American theatrical history, *A Raisin in the Sun* is disturbingly prophetic. Just as the romantic heroism of her characters and the wit of her dialogue blur the play's contradictory presentations of class, so they also distract us from Hansberry's perception of the oppression of women. To be young, gifted, black – and a woman – was perhaps too much to contain in one play or one life. *A Raisin in the Sun* raises the curtain on the complex interaction between racism and sexism but it lowers it quickly, as if to warn the audience that such chaos lies on this terrain that more clearing of the land must occur before such territory can be encompassed on stage.

Lorraine Hansberry died of cancer in 1964, leaving it to others to struggle with the questions she had raised. Other American women playwrights would indeed pick up her challenge. In the meantime, however, in Britain Joan Littlewood, Shelagh Delaney and Ann Jellicoe were simultaneously bringing parallel concerns to the stage.

Although Joan Littlewood's impact on the theatre was not felt until the 1950s, she is a woman of the same age and generation as Lillian Hellman. The same year – 1934 – that Hellman's *The Children's Hour* appeared on stage, Littlewood was beginning her Manchester-based Theatre of Action with Ewan McColl, the first of many attempts Littlewood would make to create a political theatre whose form subverted conventional modes and whose audience was the marginal people for whom West End or Broadway theatre would be ideologically and economically absurd. Except for their common concern with women, the notions of theatre embraced by Hellman and Littlewood were antithetical, and strains of each's approach as well as the tensions between the two modes continue to be present in feminist drama.

Littlewood saw most theatres as museums for dead drama. The Theatre Workshop that she established after the Second World War, and which moved to a permanent home in East London in 1953, was intended to 'get to the people who don't normally go to the theater'[4] by creating experiences in which audiences had fun and were engaged by the presence of the actors. With the exception of one work, *Oh What A Lovely War*, produced in 1963, Littlewood's role was that of director, producer, discover and shaper of scripts written by other authors. But her emphasis on music, her particular use of improvisation, her experiments with audience involvement shaped the plays she directed and set the precedent for the anecdotal, comic and ebullient style that was to become characteristic of much later feminist drama. Like the feminist dramatists who followed her example, although Littlewood did not put it precisely in these terms, she believed the personal was both theatrical and political. It was on the streets with adolescents or in prisons where she suggested that wardens became prisoners and prisoners wardens, that she believed the most exciting theatre was to be found.

The script most fully attributed to Littlewood, *Oh What A Lovely War*, was a success in London and has been reproduced frequently since its initial 1963 production by the Theatre Workshop. In the published version of the play, authorial credit is carefully and precisely given to the whole company, and the collaborative nature of the play's creation is stressed. Littlewood's own name then appears as director of the company. My intention here in talking about this work 'as Littlewood's' is not to refute that collaborative method; to the contrary, we should note the public tendency to attach the name of a single author to a play even when every attempt has been made to emphasise and assert collaboration. Here and elsewhere I yield organisationally to that inclination but urge that we recognise it as an incomplete acknowledgement of 'credit'.

The initial production of *Oh What a Lovely War* was staged as a multi-media event, a mixture of effects drawn from circuses, pierrot shows, newsreels, music-hall entertainments, slide shows and non-realistic theatre. Set during the First World War, the show within the show is controlled by a Master of Ceremonies who literally calls the tunes – songs drawn from a variety of European nations – and the scenes. The sequence of events from the war itself lends some chronological continuity to the play, but its structure is not that of fluid narrative but of montage: in a brief scene, a Frenchman, a British soldier, the Kaiser, Moltke, and a Luxembourg soldier each comment on the invasion of Luxembourg; bits of various national anthems are then played, a newspanel flashes Britain's declaration of war with Germany, and eight slides are screened depicting British and then German civilians enlisting for war.

Oh What a Lovely War is a play about war and not about women, yet important aspects of its strategy mark the way towards feminist drama. The points of view of the female characters are central to the play's illumination of the horrors and absurdities of war. It is not that the women have the 'correct' or more sensitive understanding of the ugliness of war; to the contrary, they are as burdened by and susceptible to the seductions of war as are the men. But in the voices of the women we hear the false notes of praise for war's creation of virtuous men, and we hear the truth of the grotesque sufferings imposed by war. Notably, the female voices in the play become more and more present as the show moves towards its conclusion and the end of the First World War.

The indirect affect of Littlewood on feminist theatre was also present in her support of women artists and, in particular, of the playwright Shelagh Delaney. Delaney, at eighteen, epitomised the kind of resource Littlewood felt was crucial for any authentic theatre. Reared in a working-class industrial environment in Salford, in the north of England, Delaney had dropped out of school at sixteen and written *A Taste of Honey*, the play she brought to the Theatre Workshop, because she was convinced she could write more convincing drama than she had seen on stage.[5] The Theatre Workshop revised and tightened the play in rehearsal; later, it moved to the West End and Broadway, was made into a film, and brought its author instant acclaim as a major new figure in British drama.

A Taste of Honey is a play about women; its greatest weakness is in its conception of the male characters who, with one exception, function to forward the plot but are incidental to the lives of the women. Like many subsequent feminist dramas, the two central characters are a mother and daughter. *A Taste of Honey* neither assumes nor sentimentalises this bond. Helen, the mother, is described in the opening stage direction as a 'semi-whore'. Her daughter, Jo, at seventeen, has a caustic wit, an untrained talent for drawing, and neither desire nor ability to imagine the world beyond the moment and the 'comfortless' flat where she lives. Near the end of the play, Jo poignantly summarises to her friend, Geof, her relationship with her mother: 'You know, I used to try to hold my mother's hands, but she always used to pull them away from me. So silly really. She had so much love for everyone else, but none for me.'[6]

The mutual acknowledgement that defines genuine love occurs between Helen and Jo, but each resists and conceals her affection, and Helen does her best to deny responsibility to and for her daughter. Early in the play, Helen decides to marry her latest lover, a heavy-drinking man with money in his pocket who sees women only as objects of his desire. She marries Peter for fun and to escape the squalor of her life with Jo. Literally deserted, Jo takes up with a black sailor who seals his proposal of marriage with a cheap ring and takes off for his next voyage, unknowingly leaving Jo pregnant. Jo's friend Geof, an art student whose only prior sexual experience has been with other men, moves in with Jo to nurture her through pregnancy.

As Michelene Wandor has commented, *A Taste of Honey* is 'rooted in domestic, female-centred experience', and thus presents a very different world from that usually seen on stage, at least before the 1970s.[7] More precisely, the play's activities are those of the daily life of ordinary working-class people, and central to that life is the struggle involved in every aspect of the 'domestic'. Interaction between the characters is mediated by food, clothes, cleaning, sleeping, health – the most mundane and elemental necessities of daily life, but also those aspects of life usually dismissed simultaneously as trivial and as the unique concerns of women.

In contrast to some more recent feminist work that dwells on the menial and repetitious qualities of such activity, Delaney exploits this context to reveal her characters' strength, ingenuity and vulnerability. Helen and Jo each make a series of decisions that clarify what decision-making is about for many people and especially for women. Knowing that her mother will be off with one man or another for Christmas, Jo invites her first 'boyfriend', a black sailor (whose transitory role is underlined by the absence of any name for him in the script) to spend the holiday with her. Her invitation is in part motivated by loneliness but there is also a simple desire identical to that in her mother to enjoy the moment when it presents a possibility of pleasure. 'I may as well be naughty while I've got the chance', she declares to the sailor. Neither Jo nor her mother are presented as hedonists or 'bad' women. The paradox in the play's strategy is that while much of what these women say and do is outside the bounds of assumed social mores for women, the consistency of their behaviour and their lack of surprise at each other's acts normalise their world even for the middle-class spectator.

As much as Jo and Helen defy stereotypes of women, Jo's friend Geof challenges conventional images of men. Although Helen is repulsed by his nurturance of Jo and his assumption of housekeeping tasks, we are not allowed to do so. Geof's role resists assumptions that effeminancy equals weakness and thus explodes a male stereotype. What we see of him is a young man who is able to be responsible to another without demanding anything in return, who loves Jo and would like to be loved in return but does not expect any payment for his caring. His desire to marry Jo is neither inauthentic nor pathetic; he obviously likes her wit and lack of affectation, the same qualities that draw the audience to her. Helen's rejection of Geof as a 'cretin' and Jo's inability to love him in a 'marrying' way reveal more about the inadequacies of their points of view than about Geof.

The importance of context and point of view to this play is apparent when one compares Littlewood's initial production with more recent renderings. The Theatre Workshop production of *A Taste of Honey* persistently undermined the naturalistic inclination of the dialogue, setting and plot. A live jazz trio played intermittently throughout the show, and was acknowledged by the actors-as-characters. Moments of passion, confusion and sadness were extended and articulated through bits of songs sung by the characters. The interplay between music and words, musicians and actors provided a context in which the barrier between actors and characters, stage world and audience could be penetrated.

At one moment in the Theatre Workshop production, Jo came fully downstage and addressed her 'character's' lines to the audience, not as a Hamlet-like soliloquy, but as the words of the actress that momentarily coincided with those of the character. The effect was at once to hypnotise and perplex the audience, but it also set up a context in which the actress playing Helen could address her near-final lines 'I ask you, what would you do?' to the audience. Early in the play, Helen had told Jo that she didn't go to the cinema or the theatre because 'it's all mauling and muttering, can't hear what they're saying half the time and when you do it's not worth listening to'. Littlewood's production was an attempt to make a theatre that would address Helen and those in the audience who shared her alienation from conventional theatre. Theatre was becoming personal and political.

Perhaps in the wake of too many such gestures towards audiences, and hesitations, including my own, about the breaking of the wall between performers and spectators, recent productions of *A Taste of Honey* have rigorously maintained the 'fourth wall'.[8] There is a potentially destructive ambiguity in the spectator's role when confronted with a challenge from someone who bears neither the responsibility of character nor of a 'real-world' person. Yet in presenting *A Taste of Honey* as a conventional realistic drama as was done in the film and more recently in the New York Roundabout Theater production (so successful that it was moved to Broadway), many of its most striking challenges to sexual politics are lost. The play becomes a poignant story of a hapless young girl, her brief-lived love affair with a black man, her separation and reunion with her mother. Helen's dismissal of Geof is not necessarily a sign of progress, but it is difficult to call this act into question in a straight, realistic production. The importance of *A Taste of Honey* lies in the degree to which the audience feels the weight of Helen's last question: 'what would you do?' This can be, as it was for Littlewood, a political act that shifts responsibility from the stage to the audience.

Delaney's only other produced theatre piece, *The Lion in Love*, was a commercial failure. First produced in 1960, and rarely re-produced, *The Lion in Love* is none the less a confirmation of Delaney's ability to transform both the structure and the point of view of contemporary drama. The play is a vivid example of theatrical naturalism, and as such rearticulates the differences between realism and naturalism. Realism most frequently is set in a living room, is concerned with psychological revelations about a small group of middle-class characters, and is tightly bound to plot. Naturalism tends towards more public spaces where larger groups of working-class people and social 'outlaws' divide focus. It is the behaviour rather than the hidden motivations of these people that is at issue, the community interacting with social and physical environment that is displayed and examined.

The working-class street-market setting of *The Lion in Love* is not, then, a setting without precedent, nor is the dispersion of focus among a number of characters a unique theatrical convention. But the particular attention paid to women in this world and to the texture of relationships between women and men does reinform the naturalistic mode and foreshadows a number of feminist plays of the seventies. As in *A Taste of Honey*, Delaney again is concerned with a mother and daughter, Kit and Peg, but in *The Lion in Love* the eccentric, alcoholic mother, Kit, is the main source of energy, both constructive and destructive, for the community she inhabits.

Kit's daughter, Peg, acknowledges the complexity of her mother's role in an extraordinary tale she tells to her grandfather near the end of the play. At the beginning of Peg's tale, a King and Queen play their conventional gender roles. The King does his 'Kinging in the daytime and his Queening in the night', and then goes off to war. Unlike the virtuous Queens of old, however, this Queen becomes frustrated waiting around for her husband and goes off with the 'West Wind' for a fling. The story ends with provocative ambiguity: bored with his conquest, the West Wind dumps the Queen and the child he has fathered, and:

> when the Queen realized that her husband the King had caught up with her she felt so ashamed of herself that she ran away with her child and jumped off the edge of the world, straight into the sea. And as soon as she touched the water she was changed into a great rock.[9]

Peg's tale expresses a wish that her mother feel shame, but it also visualises her mother – the barely disguised Queen – as a 'great rock'.

This resistance to the reduction of male and female roles to either old paradigms or new clichés is the driving force of *The Lion in Love*. Kit embodies a wonderfully feminist version of dramatic irony: she knows, as the men in the play repeatedly avow, that men find women to be 'funny things' and obstacles to their pleasure, and she knows that therein lies not weakness but strength – for herself, her daughter, and all of her 'daughters' in the audience.

The recognition of female power, particularly in contexts where men attempt to exploit or demean women, is an important thrust of Delaney's drama. The other well-known English woman playwright of this period, Ann Jellicoe, also found dramatic power in transforming the perception of women's weakness into a revelation of strength. For Jellicoe, however, strength is too often dangerously linked with violence and power, and women as well as men sustain such confusion.

This concern is apparent in each of Jellicoe's eight original produced plays (she has also done adaptations), but is most evident in her pageant *The Rising Generation*, commissioned by the Girl Guides Association in 1957.

Asked to create a theatrical piece for at least 800 girls and 100 boys, Jellicoe scripted a spectacular entertainment that draws on a long and buried tradition of pageants created by and for women. Looking both backwards and forwards in history, Jellicoe incarnated the 'monstrous regiment of women' that had first appeared in a misogynistic sixteenth-century pamphlet by John Knox. (Twenty years later, a company of feminist theatre artists would take 'Monstrous Regiment' as their name.) The regiment of women is led in the pageant by an enormous half-masked mother figure who looms over the other players urging the extermination of men and the conquest and control of the world by women. While satirising the extremes to which a women's movement might go, *The Rising Generation* presents a ritualised world in which women, inspired by the power of 'the mother', chant 'Shakespeare is a woman. . . . Robin Hood she was a woman', and condemn men: 'Men are black. Men are thick. Men are tall. Men are strong. Men will tear you, beat you, eat you. When you're older you will know.'[10] Mother, however, is as dangerous as any man infused with power, and when she uses the Bomb to defeat the rebellious girls who have now joined with boys to defeat her, the young people transform the entire outdoor playing area into a spaceship, a new world in which they can escape the tyranny of mother and perhaps of their own previous antagonisms.

The Girl Guides Association did not approve Jellicoe's script, and *The Rising Generation* was only produced in unsuccessful reduced form in London in 1967. The parody of feminist claims to a place in history, past and present, is unclear in its intent. *The Rising Generation* does not allow for the experience *of* rising, for the necessities of asserting strength and taking power before weakness can be admitted and power shared. Because of this, it is a peculiarly avant-garde piece of feminist theatre, a ritual drama that can literally and figuratively only leap into the air and transcend the real world in which it occurs.

Jellicoe's *The Sport of My Mad Mother*, written a few months before *The Rising Generation*, presents similar difficulties. This play, too, anticipates feminist theatre vividly in its embrace of a mythical female figure and the celebration of ritual. The 'mad mother' of the title is inspired by the Hindu figure Kali who is at once a figure of destruction and creation. In the ancient myth Kali rejects her son who castrates himself with a stone knife; in Jellicoe's play, the mother-figure, Greta, casts away the boy, Cone, who clings to her, then gives birth to a symbolic doll-child. As in *The Rising Generation* the strategy is not coherent. Greta, the mad mother, is a remote, bizarre, tyrannical and isolating figure, and her symbolic pregnancy only names but does not emotively convey the attractive, fruitful side of her character. To say that the play shares with feminist dramas a near-obsession with the mother role is not to claim that it is a feminist play, although like Harold Pinter's *The Homecoming* or Eugene O'Neill's *Long Day's Journey into Night*, *The Rising Generation* does contribute to the feminist endeavour to subvert assumptions of 'natural' gender role behaviour.

The Sport of My Mad Mother is none the less both adventurous and prophetic of feminist dramatic strategies. Jellicoe accurately describes her work in a preface as 'an anti-intellectual play not only because it is about irrational forces and urges but because one hopes it will reach the audience directly through rhythm, noise, music and their reaction to basic stimuli.'[11] During the same period, male playwrights like Samuel Beckett, John Arden, Harold Pinter and Edward Albee were also dislodging the logical continuity of the realistic well-made play, but each of these playwrights purposefully appealed to the educated mind, to the intellect. In contrast Jellicoe sought a stage world that must be experienced as irrational and hostile to the manners and modes of intellectual life. Her characters are 'Teddy boys', a rough street-gang; they eject sound as opposed to speaking dialogue, and their interactions and shifts of mood are continually mediated by an on-stage musician who is more in the foreground than background of the piece. Jellicoe's attempts to evoke feelings rather than to describe them, to 'release emotions' in characters and audience and to assault the tyranny of intellectual discourse, are consistent with many feminist arguments of the sixties and seventies.

Jellicoe's own description of her next and most famous play, *The Knack* (1961), asserts its continuity with the two earlier works in its refusal to narrate action. But although *The Knack* struck reviewers and audiences alike as daring and innovative, it is unquestionably more accessible in its language and context than either *The Rising Generation* or *The Sport of My Mad Mother*. *The Knack* shares with Jellicoe's other plays an exuberant, almost exhausting energy and the presentation of a world aggressively dominated by men. In contrast to *The Sport of My Mad Mother*, however, *The Knack* does have a series of episodes that lead inevitably from one to the other; it has, in other words, a plot.

The difficulty in considering *The Knack* as a predecessor to feminist theatre lies directly in its plot. The 'knack' referred to in the title is most explicitly the male ability sexually to seduce and conquer women. One of the three male characters, Tolen, has 'the knack' and exhibits and exploits it. A second male character, Colin, admires Tolen's 'knack' with women and attempts, mostly in vain, to acquire it. The third of the men, Tom, has a genuine knack with people but has an honest disdain for the seductive talents his fellows so treasure. The three men share a house into which blunders an ingenuous seventeen-year-old woman named Nancy. Most of what follows is predictable. At a pace that the spectator experiences as something like a film run at fast forward, Tolen 'puts the make' on Nancy, Colin tries futilely to compete, and Tom tries to coach Colin, undermine Tolen's efforts, befriend Nancy and entertain those on-stage and off.

The unexpected turn of events in *The Knack* does not occur until Act III. Having suddenly repulsed Tolen's aggressive overtures at the end of Act II, Nancy recovers in Act III insisting that she has been raped. Since Nancy has not been alone with any of the men since her initial appearance, it is perfectly clear to them and to us that her accusation is an invention. It also becomes evident that she is not deluded but has grasped a source of power over both Tolen and Colin. Her accusation confuses the men; it threatens Tolen's sense of reality and inflates Colin's ego since she vacillates in her identification of her attacker. Her claim that she has been raped also presents the real threat that she might take her charge to the police.

In performance, this transition from seduction to 'rape', from male domination to female control occurs so rapidly and maniacally that the spectator feels transported to a mad and dizzy world where anything might happen next. My summary of the plot of *The Knack* is inadequate to the play's strategy in part because the dialogue is almost always funny and in part because the script is structured to necessitate improvisation. All four characters hit words at each other like tennis balls, but, in addition, they are constantly moving, tumbling, climbing in and around the relatively bare space and each other. More than in many plays, improvisation is used both as a performance process and as an implementation of theme: part of Tolen's skill is his ability to improvise with each new woman he meets, and Colin's inability to do this is his 'failure'. It is Nancy, however, who arrives at the most successful improvisation: she has examined her situation and created a surprising, spontaneous and successful response that places her for the first time in a position of power. In the face of the male reliance on reason and scheming, one tool women can effectively use, the play suggests, is improvisation.

This thrust of *The Knack* is both inspiring and provocative. What is less clear and more troubling is just how the audience is to think about male or female power and how we are to consider the act of rape. *Reading* the script, one can infer an argument that aggressive, manipulative sexuality is as harmful as rape itself, and that almost everyone, male and female, has a distorted, inhumane notion of sex. The script also suggests that no matter in whose hands, power is a tool of manipulation, most easily employed to turn people into objects when sex is the mediating factor. But in performance, the aura of overt libido emanating from all the characters is so strong that it tends to seduce the audience towards a wish to see some sexual act performed. And in performance, the intense energy of the men could easily make the audience, especially the women, welcome Nancy's accusation simply as an act that balances power relationships. Supported by the wit of the dialogue, the play deters us from taking rape seriously; it, indeed, allows us to think of rape as a joke.

The Knack confronts us with sexuality, gender roles, power and control, yet it does not leave us with any transformation of attitudes towards these issues. Similar problems haunt Jellicoe's two subsequent plays *Shelley* and *The Giveaway*, neither of which was commercially successful. *Shelley*, Jellicoe's most conventionally structured drama, narrates the life of the poet Shelley, and while it teases the audience with repeated presentations of intriguing female characters, it blurs its own sporadic attempts to raise questions about Shelley's egocentric treatment of these women. *The Giveaway* is a blatant farce that ripples in and around an absurdist extension of a consumer's fantasy of winning a grand prize in a cereal contest. The caricatured family of the play does 'win', but the prize is not money or a dream trip but a collection of grotesquely enormous boxes of cereal that literally take over the stage. Consumption could be made into a feminist issue, but in *The Giveaway* as in her other plays Jellicoe misses or rejects her chance to explore how such issues have particular meanings for women.

Jellicoe's dramas raise contemporary feminist issues, but her vision is finally ahistorical and apolitical. She has perhaps best assessed her own work in saying that what she intends is no more than that the audience begin to use its imagination. But she offers no control or direction for our imaginations and thus makes the personal theatrical but not political.

Of the plays discussed in this chapter, Jellicoe's are stylistically closest to contemporary feminist drama yet they are the most vulnerable to criticisms of a dangerous sexism. None of the precursors of feminist drama fully united process, structure, characterisations and issues in such a way as to establish a coherent feminist genre. Ironically, the play that I have left until last, Doris Lessing's *Play with a Tiger*, written in 1962, does suggest a distinct and coherent model for feminist drama but has been dismissed by its author as a failure.[12]

For many women in the sixties and early seventies, Lessing's *Play with a Tiger* was a singular and treasured gift. Dozens of student and community theatre groups have produced the play, whose protagonist, Anna, bears a close resemblance to the protagonist of Lessing's novel *The Golden Notebook*. Anna is a writer in her mid-thirties who chooses to live alone despite her recognition of the loneliness she thus endures. She admits to herself and us her desire for and pleasure in men, and we witness her passionate attachment to one man, Dave, but she finally rejects him because he cannot accept her as the complicated woman she is.

Play with a Tiger's direct exploration of an adult woman's tensions between her images of herself as 'just a little ordinary girl' who 'wants to be married', and a woman who refuses to manacle herself to a man has a poignant appeal for any contemporary woman struggling with her own ambivalences. It is not, however, just the strength and vulnerability of the character that makes Lessing's drama transcend other works. As she states in her preface, her intent was not only to lead the audience to acknowledge a kind of woman who rarely appears on stage but to assault the stage itself and what she calls 'the greatest enemy of the theatre . . . realism'.

Lessing accomplishes this by beginning the play in the comforting setting of a living-room–bedroom that only gradually calls attention to the absence of familiar stage props and stage 'business' – lighting cigarettes, eating, etc. – that would suggest the 'real' world. Symbols of a sparer, more ritualised, constructed world explode at the end of Act I, when Dave and Anna begin to play a game in which the walls of the room vanish and time both moves backwards and stands still. Much of the rest of the play is a ritual of interaction between man and woman, an experiment and exploration of the histories that have at once attracted them to each other and made them utterly unable to touch each other in a sustained way.

In *Play with a Tiger*, each of the elements of feminist drama that appeared separately in the plays of Hellman, Hansberry, Childress, Delaney and Jellicoe merge to form a coherent whole. By the very nature of drama, point of view is shared among all the characters on stage. Anna and Dave's game, however, makes point of view itself an issue. We are shown the world through the eyes of both characters, but because Anna is more persistent and relentless in her 'visions', a genuine feminist perspective appears. We thus not only have a strong female character, we have a female *vision* of the world. The implicit argument of the play is that a female vision, presented on stage, necessarily rejects the enclosed living rooms and distracting details of realistic drama.

This is similar to Jellicoe's dramaturgy but goes two steps further: *Play with a Tiger* urges that women can only be fully present in theatre by assaulting its established conventions and women can only transform the society by accepting the pain of resisting traditional male–female relationships. Whether or not this potent and coherent theatrical strategy is less successful as an aesthetic and political act than Lessing's novels, as she herself believes, it was and remains a rich example and resource for the theatre of women that was to follow.

3
Megan Terry:
Mother of American
Feminist Drama

Since the early sixties Megan Terry has been a sustaining force in feminist drama, nurturing other American women playwrights and continually extending the reaches of her own plays. Captivated by theatre from the age of fourteen, Terry, now in her early fifties, has written more than fifty dramas most of which have been both produced and published. Reviewers whose attention is fixed on New York commercial successes tend to ignore Terry's work, but she has received public recognition and support over the last twenty years from numerous foundations and government offices. As playwright in residence of the Omaha Magic Theatre since 1970, she has, with the Magic Theatre's artistic director and founder Jo Ann Schmidman, been able to sustain one of America's most innovative theatres for more than fourteen years.

Terry's own definitions of feminist drama are deliberately broad: 'anything that gives women confidence, shows themselves to themselves, helps them to begin to analyze whether it's a positive or negative image, it's nourishing'.[1] Her plays, however, consistently reveal a precise criticism of stereotyped gender roles, an affirmation of women's strength, and a challenge to women to better use their own power. In Terry's plays we witness a sustained yet never repetitive development of transformation as the central convention of feminist drama. 'Transformation', she asserts, 'reveals to us an efficient universe. Nothing is lost – it's just transformed.'[2]

Born in Seattle, Washington, on 22 July 1932, Terry 'hung around' a community theatre until its director, Florence Bean James, took her in and she began to work on set construction and design. For Terry, the concept of transformation and its development as a key technique of her dramaturgy began with this early training in design and collage; she still thinks of what she does as a kind of architectural process in which she 'builds' plays.

Despite her father's refusal to pay for her education because she would not join a sorority, she took a BA in education at the University of Washington. Her studies included creative dramatics, taught by her cousin Geraldine Siks. Growing up, she had loved cartoon characters and impersonators; working with young children who naturally used role transformation in their daily play led her to think that adult plays could be written that used the same process.

Terry left Seattle in 1956 when a double bill of one of her first plays and a play by Eugene O'Neill was lambasted by local critics. She promised her father on her departure that if she had not made it in the theatre by the time she was thirty-five, she would give up and become a teacher. For the next ten years, she endured the struggles of a young, unknown playwright in New York, a life enriched and complicated in the early sixties by her association with Joseph Chaikin, Peter Feldman, Maria Irene Fornes, Barbara Vann, and more than a dozen other young actors, writers and directors who were rejecting the stylistically and commercially 'closed' theatre of Broadway to create what they soon called the Open Theatre. Many of the original Open Theatre company members had been trained by Nola Chilton, whose teaching emphasised the freeing of the individual actor's body and voice through exercises that focused on imagined objects and sensations. Even more important to the development of Megan Terry's work, however, was the structure given to daily workshops by transformation exercises originally created by a Chicago artist and teacher, Viola Spolin. Spolin's theatre games meshed perfectly with Terry's vision of a theatre in which actors created and altered the world in front of the audience, relying on their own resources of body, voice and imagination.[3]

In its first few years, from 1963 until 1966, the Open Theatre was a set of workshops, led by different members of the company, including Terry. By the spring of 1964, Terry had drafted a new one-act play, *Calm Down Mother*, inspired by her Open Theatre Workshops. That summer, on a month's Rockefeller Foundation Grant at the Office for Advanced Drama Research in Minneapolis, she revised this as well as an earlier, full-length drama, *Hothouse*, and another one-act play, *Ex-Miss Copper Queen on a Set of Pills*, written when she first arrived in New York. In that one month of Minneapolis heat, she also wrote another one-act play, *Keep Tightly Closed in a Cool Dry Place*. The three one-act plays became part of the Open Theatre's repertory and were first performed by the company in 1965 at the Sheridan Square Playhouse which the company rented for public performances.

Hothouse is unmistakably drawn from an earlier period of Terry's life and work (although it was not actually produced until 1974, by which time it seemed outdated to some reviewers). Set in a fishing village near Seattle in 1955, it is the only one of her plays that could be called a conventional, realistic drama. In contrast to most well-made modern plays, however, the central characters are women, and the world of the play is distinctively female. Three generations of women from one family inhabit a small house in which an uncountable number of house-plants seem to have taken over the living space. Ma, the grandmother of the group, is a spirited, not-so-old lady, who has 'started again' – with men, booze and life itself – so many times that she's lost count. Her daughter Roz spends much of her time drinking, swearing and making love to one man or another. Jody, Roz's daughter, is caught between the invigorating but crazy life of her female family and the naïve passion of her university-student lover, David. Each of the women has and wants her man, and much of the play revolves around the pending divorce of Roz and Jack, Jody's here-again, gone-again father.

Much like Shelagh Delaney's *Lion in Love*, Terry's *Hothouse*, while realistic in its detail and dialogue, relies little on narrative development, and instead builds a distinctively female environment. The experience of watching either of these plays has more in common with that of listening to a jazz trio than with witnessing Ibsenesque modern drama. Already in *Hothouse*, Terry's extraordinary ability to make every word a gesture is apparent. Hers is not the skill (or inclination) of the eighteenth-century playwrights who strove to differentiate characters through language; rather, more like Samuel Beckett than any other notable predecessor or contemporary, Terry's words function on stage as physical actions, as mediations that gradually change the people who speak and the relations between them.

Hothouse reveals a political coherence between the assertiveness of the language and the speaking voice. Terry's women defy expectations of ways women talk, especially to each other. Jody, Roz and Ma are ascerbic, witty and candid; they make us laugh as few female stage characters do. But they have not simply been allowed access to the male domain of verbal aggression. The lines these women speak express thoughts inseparable from feelings; these are intelligent people whose perspicacity reveals rather than conceals caring. When, at the end of the play, Roz gazes down at Jody who has crumpled into an exhausted sleep, she claims both her connection to and her separation from her daughter:

> ROZ: My glass is empty. Who's the bartender around here? . . . Don't be mad at me, Jody? Jody? I love you more than anything in the world. You hear that? You never have to do without love, Angel. . . . You were so little. Look at you now. Tall and pretty. As tall as your old lady. And a hell of a lot smarter. A hell of a lot.[4]

Hothouse none the less has as much in common with the predecessors of feminist drama as it does with Terry's subsequent work and the other plays that come to define contemporary feminist drama. Like almost all of Western drama, the strategy of *Hothouse* pivots around a covenant of expectation between audience and characters: the implicit promise is that at some point, usually near the end of the play, a recognition scene will occur in which a character reveals herself or himself in some new way to us and to another in the world framed on stage. In this process of revelation, both the character and the spectator learn something new about who each is. In the classic example, Oedipus endures a series of such recognitions and revelations, discovering step by step who he is and, in our witnessing of these illuminations, we assumedly discover something of who we are. The revelation of erotic attraction in Hellman's *The Children's Hour* functions strategically in an almost identical way.

The structure of *Hothouse* sustains this basic pattern. Both Jody and Roz are caught in elemental confusions about their own identities. Jody seeks self-definition through David's love for her, but finally discovers that she 'can't live off feelings of other people'; to find herself, she must acknowledge both her separateness and her ties to the women who have reared her. Roz, in turn, must acknowledge her identity as a mother, and must reveal her love for her daughter. That she initially does so half-drunk, with Jody asleep, is a resistance to the recognition scene and a source of partial frustration for the audience. But a moment later, as the play ends, the traditional convention is completed: Jody awakes in her mother's arms, returns Roz's embrace and welcomes the outside world to participate: 'COME IN BUGS . . . COME IN FLIES.'

Such recognition scenes at once assert and resist change. In the terms of ancient Greece, it is through such moments that one comes to 'know thyself'. This, of course, implies that there is some primary, core 'self' in each human being, and that the process of becoming a better person is one of shedding delusions and defences, of making the hidden seen. Within such a framework, progress is ironically a movement backwards in history, a matter of retrieval and purification, and, finally and essentially, a matter not of transformation of the self but of acceptance. It is the individual will that makes recognitions possible; context and relationships with others may inhibit or inspire the process but are secondary agents.

If one's goal as a playwright is to inspire radical alterations in human actions, then the 2500-year-old dramaturgical fixation on the recognition scene might well be viewed as a prison. The 1960s were a time when a major shift in the structure of drama became possible. But possibility is not the same as necessity, and for many male playwrights there was no compulsion to reject the old forms. (There are, of course, exceptions, like Samuel Beckett and Harold Pinter.) For women, or at least for women who saw that self-awareness and self-discovery were only first steps towards change, it was crucial that a new way be found. A theatre that genuinely included women had to take as a central convention, the overt display of people becoming other.

In this context, the work that Megan Terry produced in the mid-sixties was genuinely experimental, a struggle and testing of a whole new way of doing theatre. In the plays that follow *Hothouse* recognition scenes vanish, and in their place appear series of transformations. Instead of characters gradually and painfully discovering their true selves, actors take on one role only to discard that role in front of the audience for another. What was always true of theatre – that the human being could in this arena transcend her or himself – now became not just an unquestioned aesthetic principle but a manifestation of political and aesthetic struggle.

Within a short period of time in the mid-sixties, Terry produced half a dozen plays in this new transformational mode. The one-act *Ex-Miss Copper Queen on a Set of Pills* reveals its earlier roots and suggests the transition between the more conventional strategy employed in *Hothouse* and the transformational structure that would inform all of Terry's subsequent work. In *Ex-Miss Copper Queen* three marginal women meet on the street somewhere on the Lower East Side in New York City. The character known only as 'Copper Queen' is an embodiment of a dramatic transformation: as she lies half-drunk, half-drugged on a front step at the beginning of the play, we see both the naïve beauty queen that she was ten years before and the bedraggled street-walker she has become at twenty-six. As Copper Queen sips her wine and talks to the pavement – half-succeeding in animating it – two old women, B.A. and Crissie, appear. B.A., the more assertive of the two, wears three wigs, each a different colour and suggestive of a different age; each woman wears a rubber glove on one hand; Crissie wears a white lace glove on her other hand. The two women are scavengers. They salvage items of value from the garbage of the city streets, placing the retrieved items in an ancient but polished pram. Like Copper Queen, their appearances are perplexing and defiant of categorisation.

During the brief encounter of these three women, Copper Queen tells her story of decline from riches to rags, from innocence to brutal experience. Her success in a beauty contest in Butte, Montana, had transported her to New York, where she lost a second contest and became pregnant. Helpless, she yielded to her parents' plan that they rear the child as their own, while she stayed as far away as possible. The tale is of a transformation, but in this play, the alteration of character remains within the familiar mode of narration of past events. We do, however, witness a hint of a destructive form of transformation in the ironic tranquillity that emerges from Copper Queen as her various pills take effect.

As in *Hothouse*, it is not so much what happens, but the

nature of the bond established among the women that is important in this play. Each of the women is elusive, unfixed in any history or type. What connects each to the others and to us is their fierce determination to work and their pride in their own endurance. Within this very limited and particular group, collecting garbage and whoring are legitimate. Just as the pram is transformed from a traditional sentimental object to an efficient work tool, so work itself and its relation to women is at least redefined.

Terry's next three plays move more completely into the transformational mode. *Keep Tightly Closed in a Cool Dry Place* begins with an archetypical transformation in which the three male actors combine to become a machine. Consistent with Viola Spolin's urgings that change be developmental, the actors make a transition from the machine image to prisoners in a cell by moving in 'a military manner' to their bunks. During the one hour in which we witness these three men in their jail cell, we learn that all three have been convicted of murder of the wife of one of the men. In her production notes, Terry makes clear that the script is deliberately ambiguous as to whether a murder has been committed and if so, who is responsible for it. In contrast to some dramatic works, however, where ambiguity is intended as a device to challenge the audience, Terry's intention was at least as much to create a challenge to the players and directors 'to decide what matters to you'. The script stands as a score for actors who must, in Terry's words, 'come to understand that they are connected with one another by muscle, blood vessels, nervous structure – impulses felt by one member may be enacted by another'.[5] In the final sequence of the play the three men lock arms facing outwards in a circle and turn like a machine wheel chanting 'And roller and roller and roller, And rocker and rocker and rocker.' This image captures the interdependence as well as the constraints of the prison these men inhabit.

Calm Down Mother, written during this same period and often hailed as the first truly feminist American drama, embraces the transformational form even more persistently than does *Keep Tightly Closed in a Cool Dry Place*, but it is also an obvious complement to the latter work. *Calm Down Mother* calls for three women players, who are named in the cast of characters simply as 'Woman One', 'Woman Two' and 'Woman Three'. As in *Keep Tightly Closed* Terry has here moved into a theatrical style that unhesitatingly focuses on the actors; in the manner of the 'poor theatre' heralded by Jerzy Grotowski, the play is set on a bare stage, with the only props being four straight chairs. As the lights come up on the three women 'clustered together to suggest a plant form', we hear a taped speech in the voice of an amused gentlewoman describing the evolution of three one-celled creatures from passive life in the sea to rooting on the land.

At the close of this speech, one of the women breaks from the group structure, walks towards the audience and identifies herself as Margaret Fuller. The abrupt transition, different from the more flowing transformations that characterise other experimental work in the sixties, is the first appearance of Terry's own distinctive signature. The woman's brief speech also contains a quotation from Fuller that identifies Terry's own hope for women in this and other plays. 'I'm Margaret Fuller,' Woman One begins. 'I know I am because from the time I could speak and go alone, my father addressed me not as a plaything, but as a lively mind.'[6]

For most women, however, it is difficult to know oneself as a 'living mind', and the montage of scenes that follow in *Calm Down Mother* catches moments in that struggle for a variety of women characters. Structurally, each of the scenes is similar in its triangulation of interaction among three women and in a common tension between genera- tion, between mothers and daughters, symbolic or literal. In one early scene, two older women, sisters who run a Brooklyn delicatessen, become nostalgic when a young female customer enters whose hair reminds them of their own youth and their mother. In another scene, one woman lies still on the floor while her two daughters meet in a distant city and acknowledge their mother's impending death from bone cancer. This crisis allows the 'strong' sister to reveal her own vulnerability.

While Terry centres on mother–daughter relationships, she does not sentimentalise them. In the penultimate scene of the play, two sisters fight about the morality of con- traception, and their mother, after attempting to stop their argument, rejects the daughter who advocates the pill. 'You're no daughter of mine,' Ma cries, 'Pack your things.' That line resonates through the final scene in which all three actresses paradoxically declare their self-sufficiency and their identification with reproduction: 'The eggies in our beggies [*sic*] are enough ... Are enough ... Are enough.'

This last scene serves as an ironic counterpart to Margaret Fuller's assertion of the struggles to be a 'living mind', and also unites the varied transformational devices used to move one scene into another. Some of these transformations, links between sets of characters and contexts, are abrupt freezes in which the end of one scene is held, then released into a new context. Most of the transformations exploit a gesture or emotional beat to allow the passage of the actresses from one role to another. At the end of a nursing-home scene, the two patients, already objectified by their context, become mechanical subway doors, through which the third woman, the nurse in the previous scene, tries to pass. During the movement pattern, the women chant 'Please keep your hands off the doors.' What makes this transformation effective is that it picks up on one motif from the previous scene – the mechanisation of the lives of these women patients – and then creates a context in which a motif of the next scene about three prostitutes is ironically announced in 'keep your hands off'. By the end of the play, Terry has brought the audience to accept persistent change in the bodies, voices and roles of each actress. The image of three women, smiling sweetly at us while they touch their bellies, breasts and sides and chant 'Our bodies, our bellies . . . our funnies . . . our eggies' seems perfectly right.

Terry employs a number of similar devices in *Comings and Goings*, a play that like *Calm Down Mother*, was and remains central to feminist drama. Although many of the roles in *Comings and Goings* can be played by two women *or* two men, this play's tension emerges from pairings of many kinds and focuses particularly on male–female relationships. Class is not explicitly an issue here, but power and its relationship to gender roles are key issues to the conflicts that occur repeatedly in the play.

The opening scenes in *Comings and Goings* attune the spectator to the language-based transformations of this play. Like many of Terry's dramas, this one unveils the rituals that structure and inform our daily lives. The context of the opening of *Comings and Goings* is the awakening of a couple to a new day. The key lines exchanged between the two are 'Time to get up', and 'In a minute'. Stage directions suggest that this scene be repeated a number of times with the actors reversing roles and lines. In performance, actors stress the different meanings and infinite variety of interactions possible by varying modes of deliverance. 'Time to get up' can be spoken cheerfully, reluctantly or commandingly, and 'in a minute' can be a refusal, an acceptance or even a seductive invitation to return to bed.

The elemental frame for this opening scene sets up the performance strategy of displacement that structures *Comings and Goings*. Stage directions urge repetition of some scenes, and require that the entire company be prepared to play any role at any time. As many devices have been used to accomplish this as there have been performances. Some companies have labelled performers with numbers or names and put those labels in a hat to be randomly drawn by members of the audience. Other companies have used an on-stage stage manager to decide the moments when one performer will replace another and/or to decide who replaces whom. In some productions an arrow on a wheel has been spun by members of the company and/or members of the audience. Whichever device is used to provoke change, transformations occur both within and between scenes. Describing this outside of the context of a performance might lead to the conclusion that *Comings and Goings* is fragmented and disruptive in production. In fact, however, with any well-rehearsed company the continual exchange of actors, while emphasising the concept of improvisation within a frame, is accomplished very fluidly.

Comings and Goings is strikingly successful in performance precisely because its theme and its form are inseparable. It is a play about role definitions and role change which relies on theatrical role transformations to move the play forward. Each of the mini-scenes presents a moment of encounter between two people, in which the tension of change, of coming and going, is central. Individual control over the scene is a crucial issue of content as well as of performance. In one segment towards the middle of the play, for example, a waitress and customer enact a common ritual of ordering food; by the repetition and variation of interpretation, at times the waitress appears to be the servant to the customer, whereas in other presentations the customer is at the mercy of the waitress.

In addition to calling attention to improvisation, ritual and role-playing as basic elements of theatre, *Comings and Goings* stresses the particular relationship of social roles to gender roles. In most of the scenes a predictable male–female relationship sets the frame but awaits viola-tion or criticism. The restaurant scene, for example, illuminates gender roles by alternating control between the waitress and the customer; differences in inflection as well as reversal of the source of identical lines of dialogue make the waitress either servant or expert. As male and female performers replace each other within scenes, it becomes impossible to dismiss unequal power relations between men and women as 'merely' a matter of individual greed or condescension. We come to see that it is the roles we have defined for men and women that determine domination.

Again paradoxically, *Comings and Goings* is not simply a condemnation of social and gender roles in contemporary society. Indeed, the experience of the play for both performers and audience is constantly joyous. While the scenes portray a world in which human beings are persis-tently alienated from each other, unable to acknowledge each other's needs and desires, the uncertainty for any performer of when she or he will be on and each's responsibility for every role demonstrates an ensemble process in which each member is dependent on the other in a positive and constructive manner. The performance transcends the world portrayed and makes the mode of playing appealing to the spectator.

A similar juxtaposition of sharp political criticism with intoxicating energy in performance characterised produc-

tions of *Viet Rock*, the play that brought Terry fully to
public attention. Written in 1966 in conjunction with her
Saturday Workshop at the Open Theatre, *Viet Rock* was
one of the first plays to confront the war in Vietnam and the
first rock musical ever written. First performed on 25 May
1966 by members of the Open Theatre at Café La Mama
the importance of the play was at first blurred by the more
successful opening during the same season of another Open
Theatre production, Jean Claude van Italie's *American
Hurrah*. It was not, in fact, until after *Viet Rock* received
high praise on European tours that it received respectful
attention in the United States.

Viet Rock is a difficult play – both to perform and to
witness – but it gradually overcame its initially negative
response and lingered on in numerous productions, in the
growing anti-war consciousness of many Americans, and in
its dramaturgical effects on contemporary theatre. Subtitled 'A Folk War Movie', it fulfils that title both in its
obvious satire of scenes from war movies and its evocation
of known and newly created American rituals. The opening
circle, in which actors gradually rise from prone positions
like spokes of a wheel, bounce, then fling themselves
around the stage floor, typifies the explosive conjoining of
lyrical and satirical attitudes that permeates the play. The
human circle is accompanied first by a male voice singing
the lyrics of the play's theme-song 'Viet Rock' and then by
a taped voice that begins 'Things could be different.
Nobody wins. We could be teams of losers.'

Following the opening circle of *Viet Rock* is an 'instant
transformation' of the kind Terry employed in *Calm Down
Mother* and *Comings and Goings*: male actors become
baby boys and female actors become mothers who then
'lovingly' undress the males down to their underclothes.
Subsequent scenes relentlessly survey the variety of con-

texts that comprised the Vietnam war for Americans. We see army physicals, soldiers departing for Vietnam confronted by anti-war protesters, women burning in the final stages of death, soldiers parachuting into Vietnam and arriving mistakenly in 'Love's quicksand' in Shangri-La. The long central scene is set 'back home' at a US Senate hearing of the war that ends Act I with the ironic singing of 'America the Beautiful'.

Act II begins with the oral presentation of letters 'sent' between soldiers and the mothers back home. It then cuts, in Brechtian fashion, back to the American soldiers in Vietnam; male actors play the Americans, while female actors play South Vietnamese soldiers. At the end of the play, we are returned to an explosion and a circle, but this time the circle is tangled, 'the reverse of the beautiful circle of the opening image', and there is no sound but a 'deathly silence'.

Terry criticises war and the values that are a context for it. She misses no chance to note the sexism of the military: the Sergeant demeans his men deliberately by calling them 'girlies', the interchangeability of the weak is designated clearly by the casting of women as Vietnamese soldiers, and 'Mom' is perceived by the men as a correlative for sentiment. Because these gestures remind us that female attributes are commonly used derogatorily, they suggest a particularly feminist perspective.

Equally pertinent to the development of a feminist dramaturgy is the insistent sounding of song in this play. For Terry, as was the case for Bertolt Brecht, music renews the possibility of a poetic theatre, a theatre that at once engages and 'alienates' the audience. Here, and in some of her other plays, songs perform two apparently antithetical tasks: they transcend ordinary discourse through melody and metaphor while providing a frame in which the harshest sort of criticism can occur. Music intoxicates. It is capable of transforming not the actors but the audience. When that possibility is exploited as Terry and subsequent feminist dramatists rediscovered, it can be conjoined with words that lead us in our 'transformed' state to think differently about the world. It is thus difficult to refrain from singing 'America the Beautiful' at the end of Act I of *Viet Rock*, but as we do so, it is equally hard to avoid recognition of the lie this war gave to that song.

The tension and public attention provoked by the productions of *Viet Rock* and *America Hurrah* led to significant changes in the Open Theatre's structure. The company abolished its assortment of workshops and, with the help of a Ford Foundation Grant, decided to focus all its work on one collaborative effort under Chaikin's direction. With this change of direction, Megan Terry gradually moved out on her own, writing, with increasingly precise language, dramas that unabashedly questioned the American dream and its corruption in the hands of the greedy and mendacious. The domineering male power structure loomed large in Terry's *The People vs. Ranchman* and *Massachusetts Trust*, and women who were just beginning to address their position in American society welcomed these plays.

One of her most intriguing scripts from the late sixties was a television drama, *Home*, produced in 1968 by public television. The play envisions a futuristic world in which overpopulation has created small, isolated, dense communities that live in tiny cubicles from birth to death. All groups are overseen by an external controlling power that regulates everything from food to reproduction. A rare instance of a drama fully conceived for video, *Home*'s environment *is* its source of power and conflict. For the television production, fold-up beds were installed in walls, and one wall contained a large, circular television screen surrounded by cameras. Television and control were thus the medium and the message.

This apparent divergence from Terry's theatrical work retains many elements of her previous dramaturgy. While the characters remain constant throughout the ninety-minute production, the day is ritualistically divided into segments, and when Central Control commands, new activities are instantly initiated. Women dominate the internal space, both in number (of the nine on-stage characters, five are female) and in the urgency of their presence. But power ultimately resides in the male voice of Central Control, and the 'intruder' who eventually penetrates the cubicle is a man. The play ends in a rock song, reminiscent of the final songs of both *Viet Rock* and *Comings and Goings*.

Terry's next leap as a playwright came in 1969–70 with the creation of the Obie-award winning drama *Approaching Simone*. The Simone of the title is Simone Weil, the French writer and martyr who starved herself to death in 1943 at the age of 34. Terry had been intrigued by Weil since she first came to know of her in the fifties. Her goal in writing the play, Terry told one interviewer, was to place Simone's heroic spirit, her enormous will, in front of other women: '*Then* people will say, "My God, it *is* possible; women *are* free to do this and *can*." '[7]

This focus on one complex, transcendent woman is unique among Terry's works, but the playwright's signature remains vivid in the deployment of the rest of the cast, an ensemble who repeatedly transform into characters from Simone's life and externalisations of Simone's pleasures and pain. Terry's architectural, episodic style lends itself well to a biographical drama, in which the epiphanic as well as the ordinary moments of Simone's life and death

70

are equally embraced. Some of Weil's power lay in her own words and the poetry she loved, both of which Terry caresses in the play, but equally remarkable are the visual metaphors that evoke Simone's construction and destruction of herself. A familiar theatre exercise in which the entire company lifts one member takes on particular force in Act II when the entire cast suddenly appears to raise and caress Simone's body, which is wracked with both physical and spiritual agony. Each actor in the company removes and puts on a piece of Simone's clothing, in a haunting attempt to take on her pain. But no one can remove Simone's pain, and in the end the ensemble vanishes. Simone is left in a pinpoint of light that slowly, slowly fades to black.

Few theatrical images of the last twenty years have been as compelling as this last moment of *Approaching Simone*, and, for the first time, critics were fully appreciative of Terry's success. Instead of exploiting this success to turn to commercial theatre, however, Terry joined with five other women playwrights in 1972 to form the Women's Theater Council. This group, which included Fornes, Drexler, Bovasso, Kennedy and Owens as well as Terry, came together to demonstrate the existence of feminist drama and to support each other as well as other playwrights in achieving productions of plays that arose from women's visions. As a formal body, the Council was short lived, but it did serve to establish a network that has continued into the 1980s.

For Terry, the establishment of the Women's Theater Council and its successor, the Theater Strategy Group, did not suffice as an environment in which to pursue her own commitments to an experimental, community-based theatre in which women could thrive. In 1968, one of Terry's colleagues from the Open Theatre, Jo Ann

Schmidman, had returned to her native Omaha, Nebraska, where she had established a new more central, storefront theatre, the Omaha Magic Theatre (OMT). The goal of the theatre was to effect social change: 'We want to have an impact on the community of Omaha, Nebraska. We believe that change is possible here. There's responsiveness.'[8] Terry visited the OMT in 1970, and thus began a lasting association with the company. By 1974, while productions of her plays were blossoming throughout the country, she had moved her resident to Omaha, where she has remained ever since as resident playwright.

An early aim of the OMT according to Terry and Schmidman was 'to crash some barriers for women'. But at first, the company, which was and remains open to anyone who wants to participate, attracted mostly male actors, writers and musicians. Then in 1974, following Terry's move to Omaha and perhaps because of the increasing force of the women's movement, the desired feminist orientation of the theatre began to be realised and OMT was able to focus on plays about women by women.

The play that served as one catalyst for this change was Terry's *Babes in the Bighouse*, one of the first big successes of the OMT and one of Terry's most provocative dramas. Set in a woman's prison, *Babes* is a 'documentary musical fantasy' that interweaves clichéd public notions of life in a women's prison with documentary material drawn from prison interviews and visits. Songs and stories reveal the internal lives of the inmates. When the OMT performs the play, the audience is seated on at least two sides of the playing area; for the original production, audience members entered the theatre and were immediately confronted by brightly-coloured metal scaffolding arranged in two tiers to represent double-decker prison cells. The actors, who repeatedly transform from inmates to guards and matrons, address many of their speeches directly to the audience, and often more than one activity and discourse occur simultaneously. Despite moments of comic relief and the characteristic inclusion of song and dance, for the audience the experience of *Babes in the Bighouse* is undeniably troubling.

Throughout this play the prison world strains towards the audience, threatening yet reminding us that we are on the outside. The inmates first present themselves in a grotesque version of our projections of 'bad women': costumes for the opening utilise a wild mixture of corsets, feathers, long gloves, leather, spike heels and heavy make-up. The performers replace these costumes with simple housedresses and colourful band uniform jackets for most of the play, but the ambience of hostility of many kinds is sustained by the starkness and vulgarity of the language and the raw physical violence that repeatedly flashes or hints its presence. There is no comfort for the audience in the stripping of new inmates or the fight between two characters named El Toro and Jockey over the attentions of another prisoner. It is crucial, however, to *Babes'* intentions, that the most aggressive and distressing actions of the production are not predictable prison behaviours but are the stories the women tell us of their past and present anguish.

With *Babes in the Bighouse*, Terry's development of a distinctive feminist dramaturgy achieves a new force and cohesion. In a gesture similar to one Caryl Churchill would make in Britain a few years later, Terry and Schmidman cast men as well as women in the roles of the female prisoners and matrons, and by their own account this led the entire company to a more rigorous study of 'women's speech patterns, their physical and emotional behaviors and just how it is to be a woman.'[9] Here, as with Churchill's

Cloud Nine, there is no campiness or hidden grin in the performance of female roles by men; rather, we quickly accept from the all-female context of the women's prison that our perceptions of gender are based on social roles, gestures and styles.

Transformations also take on a more precise and fluid form in this play. According to the stage directions, the dominant dramatic image for *Babes* is 'How the Women Walk'. As spectators, we experience the walks of the performers as a continuous chord that permeates each scene. The walks serve as the occasion for transformations of one character to another, and they visually express the condition of being a woman 'in prison'. Changes in characters are facilitated and underlined by the physical rhythm of the walking movement itself.

Four years after writing *Babes in the Bighouse*, during which time she had written and helped produce another six plays for the OMT, Terry turned her attention to another kind of prison for women, the more pervasive confinement of the English language. Entitled *American King's English for Queens*, this 'musical in two acts' reveals the many sides of sexism in the uses and abuses of American English by a 'typical' American family. In the first act, we see the Connell family at home in their ordinary, daily rituals. The second act sharpens the focus and suggests new possibilities for a language of co-operation and genuine communication through the invasion of the family by Silver Morgan, a seventeen-year-old feral child.

The first hint we are given of the play's direction is a wonderfully funny yet tense scene in which Mom Connell insists, carelessly, on referring to a rabbit as 'he'. Jaimie, her young daughter, is confused and frustrated by the pronoun, because her mother's consistent reference to the rabbit as male contradicts her understanding that rabbits have lots of babies. Her mother never comes to appreciate the source of her daughter's distress, and Jaimie can only escape her confusion by asking 'If all the rabbits are boys, are all the cats girls?'

The most irritating character in the play is Dad who sets the drama's tones and tensions by his constant admonitions that his family must speak 'proper' English. For Dad, 'proper' means the absence of slang and the use of correct grammar, but he fails to see that within those rules language users make continuous decisions that shape the world in sexist terms. Dad does learn, however, and, by the end of the play, is able to ask 'Do you think like you talk?' The question is never explored in its philosophical intricacies, but it does lead the audience to agree that although language may initially define our humanness, the ways we use language determine what kinds of human beings we are and can be.

Like many of Terry's most recent plays, *American King's English for Queens* addresses central feminist issues in terms that are accessible to any spectator. On the page, these concerns sometimes seem simplistically articulated as when Susu, the oldest daughter, explains to her siblings that 'We'll have to think of a way we can teach her [Silver, the feral girl] to talk without making her feel that being a girl is not as good as being a boy.' But in performance, Terry's controlled use of dramatic conventions creates a more subtle context for the verbal statements. Transformations appear again, this time both to show different aspects of Mom's dreams and to demonstrate the changes in Silver Morgan. And the OMT's discovery of the possibilities of soft sculpture, of sets created out of the traditional female art of quilting, adds a meaningful, striking dimension to the spectator's experience.

American King's English for Queens is indicative of the

kind of path that Terry and the OMT have taken in recent years and of one possible route for feminist theatre. This path is characterised by the desire to engage the largest possible community and to do so through lightly comic, colourful, song-filled confrontations with social problems that concern every American family. One of Terry's most recent dramas, *Kegger*, pursues this route by confronting adolescent drinking; another OMT production, *Running Gag*, takes a number of light-hearted pokes at the current American obsession with jogging.

Neither of these plays directly addresses the economic and political structures that some feminists find it crucial to confront. For more than twenty years, Megan Terry has illuminated the lives of American women through her drama. Although she is a critic of sexism, violence, materialism and social corruption, her work does not call for a radical social revolution as much as it calls attention to the enormous strength she perceives in women, especially in the ability to will transformations. Hers is explicitly not a Marxist understanding of culture or society; in a distinctly American fashion, she protests inequality and injustice but does not analyse society in terms of class and economic oppression. But by utilising an ever-evolving set of feminist theatrical conventions and by putting in front of an audience a genuinely free ensemble that persistently emphasises the value of collaborative work and of women's work, Terry's dramas do suggest the possibility of transforming the texture if not the structure of everyday life. For Megan Terry, 'the real news is not that women are down, are victims, but that women are in good health and making it'.[10] And at least in Omaha, Nebraska, feminist drama is in good health and making it, too.

4
The Dramas of Caryl Churchill: the Politics of Possibility

In one of Caryl Churchill's recent plays, *Top Girls*, two sisters meet after a long separation and confront the differences and connections in their lives. With a quick leap of faith and imagination, one could replace those two sisters with Megan Terry and Caryl Churchill, and conjure up an extraordinary conversation about the joys and pitfalls of giving birth to and rearing contemporary feminist theatre. Like Terry, Churchill began writing plays in the 1950s and since that time has created an astonishingly large and significant body of work. Both eventually achieved an international reputation rare for women playwrights, and both have permanently altered the shape and direction of theatre through their insistent re-creation of the relationships between social and theatrical roles and gender. The one hundred or more plays written by these two women together establish the authenticity of feminist drama. Yet no spectator would ever mistake a Churchill play for a Terry play; in the contrasts as well as the similarities between their works, the complexities of the nature of feminist theatre emerge.

Born in London in 1938, the only child of middle-class parents, Caryl Churchill began writing at an early age, and was well educated by both family and schools. After living with her parents for seven years in Montreal, Canada, she returned to England, and in 1956 entered Lady Margaret Hall College at Oxford University. Churchill's first plays (*Downstairs*, *Having a Wonderful Time* and *Easy Death*) were, like many plays by Oxford-educated playwrights, produced by local theatres. And, as C. W. E. Bigsby has pointed out about many contemporary British play-wrights,[1] that meant not only that she had audiences for her early work but that she had better access to London theatres, since playwrights, theatre directors and review-ers continue to pay attention to Oxford and Cambridge.

When Churchill left Oxford, she was prepared to attempt an established path to London's theatres. A decade later, in 1972, she did arrive at the Royal Court Theatre, a haven since 1956 for aspiring playwrights. But unlike her male colleagues, she took a long detour enroute. She married David Harter, a struggling barrister, moved to the suburbs of London, had three sons, a series of difficult miscarriages, and began to write radio plays. Like many women, Churchill was engaged in a life more complex than even she acknowledged. She turned to radio both because it demanded less time away from home and because for the 'Fringe' playwright in a period before there actually was a Fringe theatre in London, radio was a good and respectable venue.

Her first radio play *The Ants* was aired on Radio 3 in 1962. As in many of her later works, the insects in this play are a resonant image of the oppressions of the individual in a capitalist society. *Ants* was followed by more than a dozen other radio plays including *Lovesick* (1966), *Identical Twins* (1968), *Not . . . not . . . Not Enough Oxygen*

(1971), *Schreber's Nervous Illness* (1972) and *Henry's Past* (1972). The corrupting power of ownership – of human beings as well as of property – is a persistent concern in these plays, many of which include astute and critical female voices. These were plays, Churchill said in an interview with Catherine Itzin, that 'tended to be about a bourgeois middle-class life and the destruction of it'.[2] But, at the time, it was not a matter of giving dramatic form to a coherent ideology or political stance: 'My attitude then was entirely to do with self-expression of my own personal pain and anger. It wasn't thought out.'[3]

The necessity of writing for the radio instead of for theatre turned out to be the mother of invention and pleasure, as it has for a number of American and English women playwrights for whom the dominantly female radio audience as well as the relative ease of production has proved to be a release rather than a constraint. Some of Churchill's radio plays were reproduced for live theatre or television and did not prove as effective. One such play was *Perfect Happiness*, in which three women sit around a kitchen table talking about how one of them has killed her husband. In Churchill's judgement, on the radio 'the unreality of it all blended. One had to use one's imagination equally to get characters and murder.'[4] Once the spectator saw the women, however, only the murder had to be imagined by the audience, and the play no longer worked.

Writing with three small boys in the house was difficult, and eventually Churchill hired a woman to help with the children so that she could write for a few hours a day. But still she would be torn 'about paying someone else to take care of *my* children, about the feeling that I could do it better'.[5] She wrote at home; the nanny would bring her tea and her youngest child in mid-morning, and she would want to stay with him. The pressure she imposed on herself to produce was also a strain: 'I felt guilty if I did not accomplish something while I was paying someone else to baby-sit.' Then, when her youngest child was two, the nanny moved away; Churchill decided not to hire a new sitter: 'All the old nagging questions [reappeared] of what's really important. Are plays more important than raising kids?' She did not resolve the question but continued to grab moments to write at weekends and occasional evenings. As a result of these constraints, she often wrote very quickly. Many of her plays grapple with the nature and valorisation of work and suggest that what emerged from this period in her life was the understanding that a key problem for women is the acknowledgement of a variety of activities as work.

The pattern began to change after the production of *Owners* by the Royal Court Theatre Upstairs in 1972. Churchill wrote *Owners* in three days: 'I'd just come out of hospital after a particularly gruesome late miscarriage. Still quite groggy and my arm ached because they'd given me an injection that didn't work. Into it went for the first time a lot of things that had been building up in me over a long time, political attitudes as well as personal ones.'[6]

Owners is an elegant, terrifyingly dark comedy. The double epigraph to the script aptly remarks the opposing and equally vital forces in the world of the play; aggression and passivity, the Christian work ethic and Buddhist tranquillity, destruction and creation struggle for the same terrain:

> Onward Christian Soldiers,
> Marching as to war.
> (Christian hymn)

Sitting quietly, doing nothing.
Spring comes and the grass grows by itself.
(Zen poem)

In these citations, as in the dramatic worlds Churchill persistently creates, modes of experience that we usually deem distinct or antithetical converge within one frame. As she asserts in the preface to *Traps* (1976), her attraction for theatre is founded in its ability to realise the impossible.

Aesthetically and politically, *Owners* is a discomforting play from its opening scene to its very last lines. After twenty-five years, Clegg, a butcher, is reluctantly closing his shop, yielding to the unchallengeable success of both a nearby supermarket and his wife's career in real estate. His opening lines are addressed to a woman customer:

> CLEGG: Lovely day dear. Been sitting in the park in the sun? I know you ladies. Twelve ounces of mince. And what else? Some nice rump steak dear? You don't keep a man with mince. No? Twenty p, thank you very much. Bye-bye dear, mind how you go.

The conventional paternalism of these lines and the nostalgic familiarity of the butcher shop are immediately undermined by the entrance of Worsely, whose most striking feature is his heavily bandaged wrists. With a casualness that must bewilder any spectator, the two men discuss Clegg's plans to kill his wife and Worsely's most recent, unsuccessful attempt to kill himself. The dialogue yields no clues to the audience as to whether Clegg will actually try to murder his wife, but there is no doubt that the *conversation* itself is serious and threatening. Clegg speaks unselfconsciously what most women would dismiss as their most exaggerated fantasies of male attitudes. His wife, Marion, he declares to Worsely, is his property: 'It's very like having a talking dog, and it's on the front page at breakfast, the radio at dinner, the television at night – that's mine, look, that's my clever dog. But a time comes when you say, Heel. Home. Lie down.'

Enter Marion, well-heeled and talking, but unquestionably no one's dog. She takes over the scene and the men with such assurance and relish that any conventional sympathy for her we might have anticipated instantly vanishes. 'I know very well it's a sad moment,' she tells Clegg as they close the doors for the last time to his shop, then adds, 'I can't be a failure just to help.'

Scene two of *Owners* abruptly shifts to a small dishevelled room in the damp, crowded flat of a couple named Alec and Lisa. Moments before, a burglar has left the flat in chaos. (As with the other six settings called for in *Owners*, each of these locations is minimally indicated and permanently on stage as adjacent pieces of what we will come to see as a whole world.) In Alec and Lisa, we meet the inverse of Clegg and Marion. Marion and Clegg are childless; Lisa and Alec have two children, with a third conspicuously on the way, and Alec's senile mother lives with them. Lisa at first appears to fulfil a stereotype of a sentimental, nagging, working-class woman, although as the play unravels, her conflicts about mothering and her challenges to Marion and Clegg's callousness make her a potent character whom we cannot dismiss as parody or cliché. But if Lisa is initially the female counterpart to Clegg's male beast, Alec is the antithesis not only of Marion but of any available male type. Educated and a skilled glazier, he holds no salaried job, not because he is unable to find outside work, but because he prefers to stay at home taking care of the family and domestic chores. He is a man with a perfect absence of desire, either for property or for control of others.

Attempts by others in the play to reveal Alec's passivity as inherently aggressive are repeatedly thwarted. Alec retains his moral autonomy while rejecting all obligations to social convention.

The entanglements of these characters explode on the audience in a series of small bursts: Marion persuades Alec to make love; later, in full view of the audience, Clegg and Lisa take their revenge in a grotesque scene of copulation; Lisa gives her baby to Marion and Clegg, then retrieves it; Worsely sets fire to Lisa and Alec's apartment building and Alec and the baby die in the fire as Worsely shoots himself in the head but remains unscathed.

Perhaps because both class consciousness and farce are more familiar objects and modes of discourse in Britain than in the United States, London reviewers found considerable merit in *Owners* while the short-lived American production was consistently dismissed as another derivative 'absurdist' play. *Owners* has neither the despair nor the hollow cynicism so characteristic of much modern theatre, nor is its presentation of the contiguity of possession of persons and property, of capitalism and sexism, far removed from 'real' life. The wit and sense of humour in Churchill's dialogue and the playful punctuation created by Worsely's repeated appearances in the bandages of his unsuccessful suicide attempts disguise the work Churchill demands of the audience but it would be a mistake to underestimate her challenge. The script avoids psychological explanations. Churchill shows us that people do not know why they do any particular act. This means that we are not allowed the superiority of greater knowledge than those on stage and that we are asked to pay attention despite the absence of the familiar dramaturgical conventions of irony or suspense.

There is no space in this play for sentimental empathy for

women or working-class people, nor are we allowed the satisfaction of rage at easy polarities. Like Terry and other feminist dramatists, Churchill divides our attention among the five characters, refusing a hierarchy of interest or role; she also curtails each scene so as to avoid sustained concern for any character. *Owners* leads the spectator to admit that our interest in the characters is dependent on our own limited and embedded expectations of what it means to be a man or a woman, and what it means to be a woman and a man in a relationship. Were Marion a man, her aggressive authoritarianism would be admired by most of those within the play as well as many in the audience; were Alec a woman, his lack of aggression and contented domesticity would hardly be thought of, as it is by those within the play, as mental illness. Churchill is not urging that women take on men's roles but that men and women respect and care for each other *as other*, not as extensions or reflections of themselves. It is not gender that distinguishes each character from another in *Owners* but the essential state of being human and the particularities of the individual.

This is a tricky political stance, vulnerable to criticism like that of Michelene Wandor who remarks that Marion 'appears to validate male fears of female sexual power'.[7] But in a society whose values were more like those of Alec, Marion's greed and narcissism would be as despicable in a woman as they are in a man. That Alec dies in the course of behaving as if such a society could exist is an admission that, even in the theatre, a new kind of hero is a fragile creation. But that he exists at all is a sign of possibility. The vision of *Owners* is of a society in which the prison of sexism can only be eliminated by radical changes in men as well as in women.

The London and New York productions of *Owners* elevated Churchill to the status of 'promising playwright', but did not significantly alter her work or work habits. During the next two years, she wrote the successful radio drama *Perfect Happiness*, and a television drama *Turkish Delight*, but she was increasingly frustrated by the disruption of her concentration. Painful miscarriages led her and her husband to decide that he would have a vasectomy. Then, in 1974, they agreed to try a radical change in their environment to give Caryl a chance to focus on her writing. The entire family packed up for a six-month long trip to Africa and Dartmoor: 'me living with David and coping with things so that he could work for ten years, so why didn't he take time off to do what I wanted to do?' Caryl returned from their exodus with a script of *Objections to Sex and Violence*, which was produced in January 1975 at the Royal Court Theatre. By focusing on two middle-class sisters, one of whom rebels against her background by becoming involved in political terrorism, the play reveals the frustrations of many middle-class women, including Churchill herself, in their attempts to shatter the sexual and political repression with which they were reared. Unlike *Owners*, however, *Objections to Sex and Violence* has little theatrical life of its own and never comes together as a whole.

Rather than retreating to more conventional dramaturgy, however, Churchill pressed even more firmly against the boundaries of theatrical illusion with her next play, *Traps*, in which two women and four men live in a communal relationship that has few constraints and a continually plastic structure. The title of the play is ironic, for the characters are paralysed by the anarchy of the totally communal and therefore relativistic society they have created. The 'random permutations' of the relationships are evidence of the multiplicity of simultaneously available roles so central to Churchill's vision, but the deliberately contradictory messages in the play are so unrelieved that the drama has difficulty escaping its own spinning. We are not caught within *Traps*, but outside it and excluded from it.

Still searching for a context for her work that would be aesthetically challenging and allow her political integrity, in 1976 Caryl joined with an alternative theatre company, the Joint Stock Company, to create *Light Shining in Buckinghamshire*. Founded in 1974 by Max Stafford-Clark, William Gaskill and David Hare, Joint Stock like the American Open Theatre was committed to a collective, ensemble rehearsal process and to creating a theatre that was unquestionably political without being doctrinaire. Actors and designers as well as playwrights and directors were expected to think and talk about the texts and about themselves. In their first production, an adaptation of William Hinton's *Fanshen*, the company made the decision to create activities for rehearsal that went beyond technical innovation and that brought the playwright together with the actors in the development of the script. In what might seem to be an obvious gesture, but one that is decidedly rare in theatre, actors were repeatedly asked to describe and then show what they thought was the political point of a scene.[8] Once actors extended their interest from the conventional modern focus on what the character desires or does to the balances of power, authority and obligation in a given framework, the style of performance moved unselfconsciously towards a Brechtian epic theatre mode. Such a context was ideal for the uncompromising, non-naturalistic approach of Caryl Churchill.

In her introduction to the published text of *Light Shining in Buckinghamshire*, Churchill describes how the play evolved:

First of all, Max Stafford-Clark and I read and talked till we had found a subject in the millennial movement in the civil war. There was then a three-week workshop with the actors in which, through talk, reading, games and improvisation, we tried to get closer to the issues and the people. During the next six weeks I wrote a script and went on working on it with the company during the five-week rehearsal period.

It is hard to explain exactly the relationship between the workshop and the text. The play is not improvised: it is a written text and the actors did not make up its lines. But many of the characters and scenes were based on ideas that came from improvisation at the workshop and during rehearsal. . . . Just as important, though harder to define, was the effect on the writing of the way the actors worked, their accuracy and commitment. I worked very closely with Max, and though I wrote the text the play is something we both imagined.[9]

Four years later, Churchill told me that this process was at once exhilarating and exhausting, 'much harder work in most ways than writing alone'. The effort paid off, however, for both the production and the play were consistently applauded for clarity of vision and commitment. *Light Shining in Buckinghamshire* retained many of the stylistic elements of *Owners* and *Objections to Sex and Violence* – short, self-enclosed Brechtian scenes, furniture reduced to a table and six chairs and minimal hand-props, a non-psychological depiction of characters, and company songs that interrupt and comment on the action. But it also gave its audience a coherent experience of historical change that raised serious questions about both the past and present.

Paradoxically, although both the seventeenth-century civil war setting for *Light Shining* and the production context of Joint Stock were male-dominated, it was with this play that Caryl was first unhesitantly commended as a feminist. The most obvious source of this response was Churchill's emphatic attention to the sexual and political oppression of women in a historical period – the late 1640s in England – that is often described as revolutionary and liberating. The play insists that most corners of its world are filled with and by men, and, in a cast of twenty-five characters, only five are women. But the women in the play ably claim their space.

The most extraordinary of these women, Hoskins, is a Ranter who unshirkingly believes that the millennium is at hand and that with it will come both economic and sexual freedom. Transcendent in her faith, she names falsehood and hypocrisy as she sees it in language that respects neither sexual nor social convention; her outrageous assertions repeatedly deflate the manipulative and deceiving rhetoric of the men of state. Margaret Brotherton, a vagrant beggar, functions as our reminder of what Hoskins might be without her illusory belief in the imminent arrival of Jesus Christ. And Hoskins's faith is far from orthodox; when Brotherton protests against entering a holy meeting, saying 'No, I'm wicked, all women are wicked, and I'm –', Hoskins retorts 'It's a man wrote the Bible.' Brotherton is a victim of poverty and her own acceptance of her servile status as a woman; Hoskins is a victim of her ideology, but, at least for a time, her commitment gives her a strength unavailable to Brotherton.

Equally striking are characters identified only as 1st Woman and 2nd Woman who reveal the particular sufferings of poor women in an emerging capitalist society; precisely because of their anonymity, these women make an unsentimental appeal to our sympathy when one of them is forced by her lack of milk to desert her baby. In contrast to other images of women during periods of war, Churchill's women do not suffer because of the deaths or defeats of their men but because they have lost the most by the defeat of a genuinely egalitarian movement. In this play, as in *Owners*, there is no separating the evil that ensues from the ownership of property from the impoverishment of the lives of women. In Hoskins's vision of the world about to dawn, 'we'll have no property in the flesh. My wife, that's property. My husband, that's property.' The message is clear, more in tune with the epigrammatic assertions of other feminist plays of the seventies, and with studies of the biases of ordinary language, than with Churchill's earlier dramas.

Churchill marks and distinguishes her feminism, both in the theatrical approach to this play and in its historical perspective. To emphasise the distinct angle of her vision, Churchill urged that the characters should not be played by the same actors each time they appeared. In the original production presented at the Traverse Theatre in Edinburgh in 1976, six actors played all of the twenty-five roles and characters were presented by one actor in one scene and another in the next. Churchill's most immediate intention in using this device was 'to reflect better the reality of large events like war and revolution where many people share the same kind of experience'.[10] In addition, however, the device politicises the theatrical convention of transformations initiated in experimental theatre in the sixties and potently adapted by many feminist playwrights in the seventies. In theatrical transformations, actors paradoxically deny and reinform the magic of what Michael Goldman has called the actor-as-character by revealing rather than concealing change.[11] In transformational exercises and episodes, actors gradually and subtly alter their facial masks, vocal tones, mimed objects. In *Light Shining* as in Ntozake Shange's *for colored girls* or Megan Terry's *Comings and Goings*, the script requires role transformations to emphasise the commonality of the stories told and to refuse the old hierarchies of theatre. Theatrical transformations demand intense focus and precision and remind us that our awe of the actor derives at least in part from the confirmation that *we* can become other, that *we* can change. But transformations also assert the collective nature of theatrical performance, the interdependency of all those on stage, and undermine our often desperate desire to hook our empathy and admiration to a star – or leader. That it has been feminist theatre groups and women playwrights who have sustained, explored and extended this gesture is coherent with a more widespread struggle against male authoritarianism.

Many of the heralded gestures of Churchill's recent work can be traced back to the historical vision and transformations of *Light Shining*, yet it is in *Vinegar Tom*, her next play and the companion piece to *Light Shining*, that the perspicuity of her vision becomes most apparent. Turning again to seventeenth-century England for her setting, Churchill this time shines her light on a society whose misogyny is grotesquely expressed in its condemnation of select women as witches. In *Vinegar Tom*, a pervasive and complex terror of women by both men and women, what Dorothy Dinnerstein asserts as 'the crucial psychological fact . . . that all of us, female as well as male, fear the will of woman',[12] motivates the persecution of women as witches. The women accused in *Vinegar Tom* are 'guilty' of healing, choosing to live without men, aborting a fetus and taking pleasure in sexual intercourse. For these crimes they are first shunned and made objects of horror in the community; later, they are tortured to provoke confessions and finally hanged.

The Dramas of Caryl Churchill

Before 1976, all of Churchill's work had been created in seclusion: 'I never discussed my ideas while I was writing or showed anyone anything earlier than a final polished draft.'[13] *Light Shining in Buckinghamshire* and *Vinegar Tom* marked the departure from this mode of work. From its early stages, *Vinegar Tom* was created in collaboration with Monstrous Regiment, a feminist–socialist theatre company formed in 1975 that was dominated by women but included men. Monstrous Regiment had taken its name from a sixteenth-century pamphlet by John Knox entitled 'The First Blast of the Trumpet Against the Monstrous Regiment of Women'. Churchill was eager for the opportunity of creating with others as well as for the chance to reach a different audience from that of the Royal Court where most of her previous plays had been performed.

The result was Churchill's most accessible play and her most straightforwardly feminist work. Evidence she found in her research of 'the extent of Christian teaching against women and . . . the connections between medieval attitudes to witches and continuing attitudes to women in general' become fiercely present in the play's depiction of the suffering of each of the female characters who attempt to defy established conventions for women's behaviour. In contrast to other of her works, *Vinegar Tom* evokes empathy for a limited number of fully wrought characters, and, throughout most of the play, sexual identity is not only unambiguous but vividly polarised: women are victims of male oppression, scapegoats for the failures and impotencies that men cannot acknowledge as their own. The best chance women have, one woman in the play advises another, is to 'marry a rich man, because it's part of his honour to have a wife who does nothing'. 'Whatever you do, you must pay', warns one of the play's songs, 'If You Float':

You may be a mother, a child or a whore.
If you complain you're a witch
Or you're lame you're a witch
Any marks or deviations count for more.
Got big tits you're a witch
Fall to bits you're a witch
He likes them young, concupiscent and poor.
Fingers are pointed, a knock at the door,
They're coming to get you, do you know what for?[14]

Songs similar to 'If You Float', and a final scene in which two male professors of theology expound their biblically derived thesis that witches are predominantly female because 'All wickedness is but little to the wickedness of a woman', are the script's only attempts to disrupt an otherwise narrative and realistic style. Churchill asks that the 'professors' be played by women as Edwardian music hall gents, a gesture that at once satirises and publicises absurd convictions about women's 'nature' propagated by figures of authority. This device amuses as a coda, but much more rests, uneasily, on the songs, to be performed in contemporary dress, as a link between past and present and a means to keep the spectator at some intellectual distance from the characters. The songs, written in collaboration with Helen Glavin, succeed in shifting attention from the horror of events unravelling on stage to the contemporary oppression of women, but they are inappropriately didactic if not properly performed. Churchill attributes the failure of the songs, in productions in Northampton and San Francisco, to their presentation by characters in seventeenth-century costume. It is important for the audience to see the singers in contemporary dress in order to emphasise the continuity between present and past and to

clarify that the songs are a commentary by the performers
on the events within the play.

Implicitly throughout the play and explicitly in its final
song, addressed, sardonically, to 'evil women', *Vinegar
Tom* is not only about women but is addressed to women. A
similar strategy was apparent in the next production on
which Churchill worked, *Floorshow*, a Monstrous Regiment cabaret presentation composed by Churchill,
Michelene Wandor, David Bradford and Bryony Lavery.
With these productions as groundings, Churchill began in
1978 to work on still another collaborative project that was
to become her most commercially successful work, *Cloud
Nine*.

For *Cloud Nine*, Churchill returned to the Joint Stock
Company and a collective scripting process. From its
inception, the play was as much a challenge to the men and
women creating it as it was to become for audiences. Actors
were selected not only in the traditional terms of their
appropriateness for projected roles or their professional
skills, but on the basis of interviews in which they were
asked to discuss their own sexual identities. The original
intention was to choose a group of actors who represented a
broad spectrum of sexual experience and identity; they not
only wanted men and women, but men and women who
were gay, lesbian, heterosexual, married and single. Yet,
once the company talked, read texts on sexual politics and
worked through exercises exploring gender and sexuality,
they began to educate each other about the diversity of
sexual possibilities and to unfix these categories and their
own identifications with them.

A shared assumption that power most frequently resides
with men became a key issue for the group. They created a
game in which numbers and images (jacks, queens, etc.) on
playing cards represented varying degrees of power; red

and black respectively represented male and female. Players arbitrarily received cards assigning them numerical power as well as a sexual identity; they were then to improvise situations and interact according to their given power. Repeatedly, actors who received cards identifying them as males would assert more power than those who received cards identifying them as females; assigned gender outweighed off-stage sexual identity as well as numerical scores. The game confirmed Churchill's own tendency to avoid differentiation between interior and exterior actions. In her plays, inner 'psychological' conflicts and outer 'social' conflicts walk together, and equally, on stage.

From these games and conversations as well as from the particular stories of members of the company, Churchill created a script that both asserts the inseparability of class and sexual oppression and calls into question the rigidity of our perceptions of human beings as men and women. The first act of *Cloud Nine* is set in a British colony in Africa in Victorian times; Act II occurs in a London park in the present. The characters we meet in Act I comprise an extended family, ordered and controlled by Clive, who introduces himself as 'a father to the natives here,/and father to my family so dear'. Clive also introduces his wife, Betty: 'My wife is all I dreamt a wife should be./And everything she is she owes to me.' Clive, Betty, their children, black servant, governess and friends are all grossly exaggerated stereotypes of their given roles, or so it seems at the beginning of the play. But as the act develops only Clive continues to behave predictably: Betty, the 'dutiful' wife literally throws herself at Clive's best friend, Harry Bagley; Harry agonises over his loyalty to his friend and his love for Betty, then makes love to both the black male servant and Betty and Clive's son; Ellen, the governess, reveals that her devotion to Betty is not a matter of obligation but erotic attraction; the widow, Mrs Saunders, makes love with Clive but insists on her independence in the face of Clive's endless lust. In good comedic form, Act I ends with a wedding, but, continuing the assault on our expectations, the bride and groom are Harry, the gay family friend, and Ellen, the lesbian governess. Socially and dramaturgically, traditional structures have been at once upheld and exploded.

Churchill's requirements for the casting of these roles teaches anew the power of theatre. In *Cloud Nine*, some actors are to play roles antithetical to their 'real-world' identities or appearances. In Act I, Betty is to be played by a man; Edward, her son, is to be played by a woman, and the black servant is to be played by a white man. The young daughter, Victoria, exists on stage in the first act as a doll. Churchill's stated intent is to 'physicalise the characters' psychologically ambivalent identities'. In performance, this startling casting is not simply a momentary symbolic gesture. In keeping with Churchill's strategy, Tommy Tune, director of the New York production, firmly resisted a campy or caricatured presentation of characters. The actors cast counter to their racial or sexual identities were directed to play their parts with authenticity and commitment. In fact, when Churchill returned to New York a few months after the production had opened there she told the man playing Betty that she did not like the bits of business and hamming he had added to his performance; he saw a video tape, agreed with Churchill's judgement, and changed the performance. Churchill wanted to create for the audience an experience close to her own: at one point during rehearsals, she recalls, she had 'forgotten' that the actor playing Betty was a man, despite the fact that he was dressed in jeans and sweatshirt and sporting a full beard. Part of the point to these role exchanges was to remind the audience of how much, in fact men and women do *look* alike. Confronted with this awareness, we might rethink the categories in which we place people.

Less and more is asked of the spectator in Act II of *Cloud Nine*. Each of the actors takes on a new role, but only one character, Victoria's daughter, Cathy, is played by the 'opposite sex'. (Not coincidentally, she is played by the white male who was the black servant in Act I.) In addition, in Act II, the audience is asked to leap a hundred years in time while accepting the illusion that the characters who were in Act I have only aged twenty-five years. Betty reappears as a middle-aged woman in the process of divorcing Clive; her daughter Victoria is now a mother herself, married to a 'liberated' man named Martin; Betty and Clive's son, Edward, has grown up to be a park gardener and aspiring novelist who lives, initially, with his male friend, Gerry. By retaining essentially the same family, placed in an ostensibly different world, Churchill provides some genuine continuity for the spectator; she also extends our political understanding that over the course of the last hundred years, family structure has altered but at a slower pace than have the ornamental aspects of social life. In 1982, Victoria can end up living in a menage of five with her woman friend Lin, her brother Edward, her own child and Lin's child, all of them sharing a bed together, but parent–children relationships, domestic roles, attitudes towards work, and assertions of power remain remarkably similar to those of Victorian England.

In its imposition of metaphor on history, its condemnation of ownership and its assertion of the ability of theatre to reframe the world counter to ordinary experience, *Cloud Nine* unites many of the dramaturgical and political actions of Churchill's earlier work. Like *Owners*, *Cloud Nine* is also a comedy of manners that makes us laugh repeatedly at the recognition of our own hypocrisies. The precision of Churchill's language bites, and there is never a verbal action we cannot understand unless we refuse to.

Churchill's *Top Girls*, performed at the Royal Court Theatre in the autumn of 1982 and in New York by the same company (and, subsequently, by an American company) continues to disrupt the audience's expectations of time and history while isolating more than previously the particular complexities of women's lives. A marriage of two plays that had been struggling for life in Churchill's head, *Top Girls* complicates and extends questions about women's roles. For years Churchill had been haunted by an odd collection of dead women drawn from history, paintings and literature: a thirteenth-century Japanese courtesan, a figure from a Brueghel painting, a Victorian traveller, and Chaucer's Patient Griselda have been ghosts at the playwright's table and are now the dinner-guests of Marlene, the head of a high-powered employment agency. The extended first image of the play suggests a visual and verbal tableau of Marlene and her guests at a long formal dinner table in a private room of a restaurant. This prologue is a dramatic genealogy of Marlene's historical community.

The other drama, that has now become the centre of the play, concerns Marlene's relationships with her working-class sister, the sister's 'thick' sixteen-year-old daughter (who is eventually revealed to be Marlene's daughter), and the 'tough, high-energy' women in Marlene's employment. All of the characters in *Top Girls* are women and are to be played by women. Each of the women performers, except the one playing Marlene, plays multiple roles, connecting the different contexts and subtly suggesting a continuity in women's history. That the actress playing Marlene is the only one who does not transform is not simply a pragmatic decision but a choice that suggests the limits to Marlene's goals.

Top Girls has been praised by some reviewers for its innovative dramaturgy and denounced by others for creating too much confusion for the audience. With *Cloud Nine*, even spectators made uncomfortable by the play's polymorphous sexuality were moved by Betty's struggle to re-create herself and by her encounter, near the end of the play, with the ghost of her old self from Act I. In *Top Girls*, not only is the disruption of narrative chronology instantly disconcerting, but we are left again without a transcendent female figure. Like Marion in *Owners*, Marlene is a woman we must take seriously but she is also a woman who accepts male models of success as exemplary and is thus not someone we are meant simply to admire.

The women characters who most intrigue Churchill have no easy victory over their own constraints and terrors. Indeed, she was disturbed by a script change in the New York production of *Cloud Nine* that moved Betty's most poignant speech of self-discovery from a non-conclusive context to the end of the play where it suggests a much surer affirmation of future possibilities for women than she intended. Churchill struggled with a similar issue in relation to *Top Girls*. The two sisters of *Top Girls* are able to resolve their own conflicts over their 'daughter', but the girl herself is doomed to a miserable life in which she can achieve neither self-respect nor community with others. The daughter stumbles from her bed to centre stage in the last image of the play, and her final cry is a terrifying shriek of isolation and need. The audience is left with a sense of despair, and while this is only one of the notes sounded in *Top Girls*, it does not provide the positive inspiration that many spectators crave.

That final note of distress, as well as the unresolved class issues that it articulates are resounded in Churchill's *Fen*, produced only months after the opening of *Top Girls*. Continuing to develop her particular mode of performance transformations, Churchill constructs this play around twenty-two characters to be played by five women and one man. An archetype of feminist drama as 'landscape', *Fen*'s environment is its subject. In the opening speech, spoken by a Japanese businessman performed by a woman, we are told of the long, exploitative history of this English swampland, retrieved by businessmen from the 'fishes and eels', and owned now by 'Esso, Gallagher, Imperial Tobacco, Equitable Life', as well as a Japanese corporation.

The people who fill this landscape are the female workers of this land whose dreams, poverty and despair resound like chords evoked by the single note at the end of *Top Girls*. In a series of twenty episodes, the oppression of women as women and the oppression of women and men as workers are continually interwoven. Central to the play's strategy is the juxtaposition of many generations of these women workers. Struggles towards change are as futile for the young girls in the play as they are for their mothers and grandmothers. As the 'Girl's Song' suggests, there are no transformative models for these women who fear leaving the village but within it can only dream of being a cook, a hairdresser or a housewife. Endurance is the keyword in these lives, and the only escape is suicide.

In addition to this despondent view of past history, a number of motifs from Churchill's earlier plays recur in *Fen*. The strongest character in the play, Nell, is reminiscent of the women accused as witches in *Vinegar Tom*. Nell just 'can't think like they do', and, as a result, is viewed by others as a 'morphrodite'. As in *Owners*, the ownership of people and of property are interdependent parts of one economic system in *Fen*, but in this more recent work, the parallel is not metaphoric but literal. Sisterhood as a resource for women is acknowledged here as it was in *Cloud Nine* and *Top Girls*, but in *Fen* the insufficiency of the establishment of communities of women is more directly addressed. The group of Baptist women who support each other through miscarriages and abuse by men give each other more than each would have alone, but as a newcomer to their group perceives, these women reaffirm for each other the sense that they are all 'rubbish'.

The absence of any positive strategy to change the kind of dismal enslavement of women displayed in *Fen* seems to support the kind of criticism some reviewers make of Churchill's work. 'I'm accused,' she said when I spoke with her, 'of being both too optimistic and too pessimistic . . . and of being too philosophical and aesthetic and not sufficiently political.' Although her plays do unveil a past and present world in which women's condition is consistently one of anguish without time for reflection, Churchill's dramas themselves, like those of Megan Terry, do not accept that misery as inevitable. Her plays, especially the last three, strive to make the audience angry through language and images that empower the spectator to act outside of the theatre. At the end of *Fen*, Nell, the 'morphrodite', crosses the stage on stilts and tells us that as she was walking out on the fen, the sun spoke to her: 'It said, "Turn back. Turn back." I said, "I won't turn back for you or anyone." '

Neither, it is clear, will Churchill's dramas. In her continuing, accelerating project to revise the history of the past and the present she makes a new kind of history – of the theatre and of society – appear not just possible but necessary. To see what that future will look like we must await her next plays, but we can be certain from her past work that it will be 'Upside down when you reach Cloud 9.'

5
A Network of Playwrights

During the 1960s, while the women's movement was gradually emerging in the United States and Britain, and while Megan Terry in New York and Caryl Churchill in London were giving shape to two distinct visions of feminist drama, a number of other women were writing plays that were unhesitantly informed by their consciousness of women as women. At first, most of these playwrights were Americans, and few thought of themselves as forging a new genre of drama. Between the late sixties and early seventies, however, as each new 'feminist' play appeared, often in New York at the Judson Poets' Theatre or Café La Mama, a network evolved of women playwrights who recognised in each other's work a common cause and struggle. Six of these women – Maria Irene Fornes, Adrienne Kennedy, Rochelle Owens, Julie Bovasso, Rosalyn Drexler and Megan Terry – formalised their mutual support in 1972 with the formation of the Women's Theater Council, an organisation intended to encourage and support productions of new plays by women. Simultaneously, other threads were being woven by new women's theatre companies and playwrights whose work was inspired by both the Black Arts renaissance and the women's movement. Myrna Lamb, Tina Howe, Susan Yankowitz, Sonia Sanchez, Ursule Molinaro and Maureen Duffy among others created an assortment of plays that, when gathered together, revealed an unmistakable pattern and coherence. Together, the plays written by all these women sounded an immutable chord of presence and protest. From the perspective of these playwrights, women's plays were unique not just because they were *by* women but because they called into question basic assumptions about how human beings view their past and present roles.

Most of the women who formed this new network were born in the early thirties, grew up in the depression and war years, and began writing in the early fifties. They were adolescents in a time when images of extraordinary suffering were inescapable. The disruption of their adolescence by the struggles and explosions of the Second World War persistently manifests itself in the fragmented, achronological structures of their plays and the prevalence in their work of surreal and grotesque imagery. The influence of cinematic structure is apparent in their plays – and often in the comments they make about their work. Meaning emerges in their theatre from the collisions of characters, contexts and images rather than the sustained unravelling of plot. Their characters struggle towards truth through transformations, not through the traditional theatrical mechanisms of revelation and recognition. Whether these playwrights came from middle-class or working-class backgrounds, and they in fact came from both, the essentially stable, secure worlds of living-room realism were inappropriate to the visions they wished to stage.

Of all the plays to announce this difficult and frequently discomforting theatrical perspective, it was Myrna Lamb's *But What Have You Done For Me Lately?* that first gained international attention and established a paradigm for the feminist theatre of the seventies. By the late sixties, Megan Terry's *Calm Down Mother* and *Comings and Goings*, Doris Lessing's *Play with a Tiger*, as well as Caryl Churchill's radio dramas, had growing audiences among women and men who were 'raising their consciousnesses', but none of these plays traumatised audiences in the manner accomplished by *But What Have You Done For Me Lately?* As described by Anselma Dell'Ollio, director of the New Feminist Repertory Theater and of the first production of Lamb's play, spectators at every performance of the twenty-minute production were unusually and intensely involved in what they saw: 'Clenched fists, gnawed knuckles, heads cocked to catch every word, these were a common sight.'[1]

But What Have You Done For Me Lately? was and remains a shocking play, if only for its central conceit, in which a pregnant man pleads with a female doctor for an abortion. Utilising one of the main conventions of the evolving feminist theatre, Lamb's play depends on role reversal to make its point: a man is placed in not just any but *the* position usually assumed to be female, and his response is that associated with the uncountable numbers of women faced with the prospect of an unwanted child. The role reversal does not require the actor to play the 'opposite' sex; in Lamb's drama, a male actor plays a man. But the activities and responsibilities of that male character are radically displaced as they were to a lesser degree in Churchill's *Owners*.

Only in theatre could such a transformation of roles be accomplished convincingly, and indeed, while confounding common sense, Lamb's projection only extends traditional limits of theatrical sense. Audiences for hundreds of years have accepted the theatrical authenticity of the 'Unnatural Caliban', born not of woman, but of the witch, Sycorax; we do not have to stretch much further to accept a pregnant man, for any creature can live on stage.

Lamb's strategy, however, relies doubly on the audience's suspension of disbelief. It is not we who have trouble believing for twenty minutes that the character identified only as 'Man' is pregnant. The conflict within the play and the tension for us as spectators is evoked because *he* has so much difficulty accepting his condition and role. Lamb's point is simple and unashamedly didactic: to accept the man's arguments for an abortion in *his* case necessitates acceptance of the same arguments and conditions for women. The importance the man claims for his work, the physical pain he will suffer, his lack of preparedness for 'motherhood', the social ostracism he will be forced to endure, are the identical claims made by women who want abortions.

But What Have You Done For Me Lately? is a morality play that argues against the imposition of parenthood on any human being. Whether or not the play persuades the audience, Lamb's work has endured because it cannot fail to perturb our assumptions about 'natural' attributes of male and female life. Like Churchill's *Owners*, *But What Have You Done For Me Lately?* should also lead spectators to question our difficulty hearing some arguments unless they are voiced by men.

Unfortunately, the concept of a pregnant man is so strong that it overshadows both the subplot of this play and Lamb's other, connected dramas. Throughout *But What Have You Done For Me Lately?*, we witness not just the dialogue between the pregnant man and the female physician, but a silent sexual power game between a Soldier and a girl in which the Soldier symbolically rapes the girl; then both are wounded. This theatrical use of parallel montage, a device borrowed from film technique, extends the play's meaning to an elemental concern with violence and power between men and women. As with similar devices in Terry's *Viet Rock*, by itself this mime would be far less effective than it is here, where it is juxtaposed to the long speeches of the doctor and pregnant man.

The short plays that follow *But What Have You Done For Me Lately?* in the set of Lamb's plays called *Scyklon Z* are intended to be performed as one work. Each utilises a structurally analogous juxtaposition of didactic dialogue with evocative, distressing visual images. The Boss and The Man coldly discuss The Man's destruction and impotence in *The Butcher Shop*; they are surrounded by carcasses, hooks, knives and cleavers that are never directly mentioned but serve to mediate our understanding of the gross terror of sensuality – and of women – that controls many men's lives. In *The Serving Girl and the Lady* we witness a parallel interplay of domination and subservience between two women; their interaction is mediated by the 'female' props of a wig, fluffy apron, jewellry, a padded bra 'and/or the bustling, sweeping, scrubbing, sewing . . . of the serving girl'. Photographs or other two-dimensional representations of abnormal fetuses in over-sized laboratory bell-jars serve as the ever-present visual counter to the archetypical seduction scene played out between the austere Female Lab Director and her 'suave' successful male-god partner in another Lamb one-act play, *In the Shadow of the Crematorium*.

Each of these short plays assaults marriage, possession and ownership in all elements of life as activities that facilitate self-destruction. In few of these plays, however, are the visual and verbal gestures integrated; their mode is thus more like that of performance art, in which the spectator must create a story by combining disparate elements of setting and human behaviour, than of traditional theatre in which such connections are pre-arranged.

In contrast, one of Lamb's full-length plays, *The Mod Donna*, first performed in 1970 by the New York Shakespeare Festival, turns to a more theatrical contemporary medium, the television soap-opera, for its mediating imagery. Subtitled 'A Space-age Musical Soap Opera with Breaks for Commercials', *The Mod Donna* utilises film, video, photographs and a 'super-clichéd' living-room set to satirise the hypocrisies and futility of attempts to achieve freedom through the late sixties' versions of sexual liberation. A 'romantic' triangle, generated by master–servant roles, endures all of the predictable resolutions and conflicts of three people engaged in a superficially 'liberated' affair, including the pregnancy of the madonna, Donna. Between and occasionally within the soap-opera scenes of tawdry life among the sophisticated upper-middle class are songs and interjections by a chorus of women who protest their entrapment in the roles assigned to and accepted by women. Taking their space in between-scene commercials, the women of the chorus come to dominate the play much as commercials tell the key tales of television. The chorus has the last word in *The Mod Donna*, and that word is an acknowledgement of women's participation in whoredom and their struggle 'to prevail'. Their last actual word, repeated three times, is 'Liberation'.

For Lamb, in contrast to many American women playwrights, that call for liberation is an attack on capitalism itself as a structure that enables continued economic and personal oppression through institutions such as marriage. In *The Mod Donna* as well as in many of her other plays,

Lamb sets up overt class distinctions that parallel the unequal power relations between men and women. In a voice similar to that of Michelene Wandor and other socialist–feminists in Britain, Lamb embraces an 'ultimate revolution . . . that is the liberation of the female of the species so that the male of the species may be freed forever from supermasculine compulsion and may join his sister in full and glorious humanity'.[2]

While the stridency of her voice and the particular political vision it embraces distinguish Lamb from some of her American contemporaries, she shares with her sister playwrights a common set of images and a recognition of the appropriateness of the chorus to feminist theatre. Susan Yankowitz's *Slaughterhouse Play*, written during the same period, is yet a third feminist drama (Churchill's *Owners* and Lamb's *The Butcher Shop* being the other two) in which slabs of butchered meat provide the central visual metaphor. Yankowitz extends the metaphors of meat and slaughter to a grotesque vision of a society in which powerful white men 'literally' castrate black men and proudly sell the blacks' genitals as prize meat in their slaughterhouse. Women are absent from the power structure, and their oppression is intermingled with that of blacks and of the poor. This drama moves with a disconcerting fluidity between realistic episodes from the daily street life of black Americans to the surrealism of the slaughterhouse where the white, male Board of Directors physically and verbally relish their meaty products.

Yankowitz's fierce assault on American society draws some of its fire from her own roots in Newark, New Jersey, site of one of the worst ghetto uprisings in American history. She received her initial dramaturgical education in the mainstream of American theatre training at Yale School of Drama, but then went on to join the Open

Theatre during its later stages of development. In *Terminal*, written in collaboration with the Open Theatre, as in *Slaughterhouse Play* as well as a dozen other Yankowitz dramas, concern for and about women's roles is a constant but never isolated issue. Male and female performers transform and exchange male and female roles in *Terminal*, and images of women going 'from the kitchen to the bathroom/from the bathroom to the bedroom' or 'nibbling at the pavement/chewing at the pavement' are especially strong. Yet the script's key line, 'the judgment of your life is in your life', is equally pointed at men and women.

Anger at the multiple oppressions of class, race and sexuality is equally evident in the plays of Adrienne Kennedy, the one black woman among the founders of the Women's Theater Council. Kennedy first received recognition as one of the major voices in the rebirth of black theatre in the sixties, and then, somewhat ironically, was 'rediscovered' in the seventies as a feminist dramatist. In her work, in contrast to some more recent black feminist plays, there is no apparent conflict in the fusion of these perspectives. The central character in her best-known play, *Funnyhouse of a Negro*, is a black woman named Sarah who announced the play's intentions in her first, long monologue:

> You will assume I am trifling with you, teasing your intellect, dealing in subtleties, denying connection then suddenly at a point reveal a startling heartbreaking connection. You are wrong. For the days are past when there are places and characters with connections with themes as in stories you pick up on the shelves of public libraries.
>
> Too, there is no theme. No statements. . . . I might try to join horizontal elements such as dots on a horizontal

line, or create a centrifugal force, or create causes and effects so that they would equal a quantity but it would be a lie. For the statement is the characters and the characters are myself.[3]

Such a transparent, prosaic statement seems more suited to an essay about drama than to the stage itself. In performance, however, this speech occurs after an intricate and enigmatic visual opening and a brief and laden exchange between two expressionistic representations of Queen Victoria and the Duchess of Hapsburg. The play's first gesture is a full-stage cross, in front of a closed curtain, by a woman dressed in a white nightgown; her face is concealed by a pale yellow mask with no eyes. The woman carries a bald head in front of her. When the frayed, white satin curtain opens, it reveals a monumental bed, sharply focused in white light, over which fly great black ravens. Queen Victoria and the Duchess of Hapsburg stand at each end of the bed, costumed in the same 'gnawed' white satin as the curtain and masked like the woman who began the play. Neither woman moves during the opening dialogue which plunges instantly to an acknowledgement by both the Duchess and Victoria that the knocking they hear is the sound of the return of the father whose intent is to rape them as he raped their mothers.

Stylistically, we are in the world of August Strindberg's dream plays, an imagistic, non-narrative theatre in which half-conscious memories and longings magically materialise in invented forms. But in a reverse of most twentieth-century uses and abuses of such expressionistic techniques, Kennedy leads us not from reality to illusion but interrupts the dream. Having made the audience struggle to make connections in the opening moments of the play, she now warns us to avoid such attempts and to insure that we do so, she proceeds, through her central, autobiographical character, to tell us everything we might want to know about the play and its main character. Continuing in the language of an essay, Sarah goes on to tell us that she is a black, middle-class English major who writes poetry, dreams of Queen Victoria, and will have white friends. 'I find it necessary,' she announces, 'to maintain a stark fortress against recognition of myself.'

Sarah has built her fortress by removing herself from the world and human relationships. Her fortress, however, cannot protect her from the 'beasts' inside, and as she talks the irreconcilable parts of herself recommand the stage. The prose monologue, then, is just one of Sarah's voices, and, while on the page it has the force of clarity, on stage it is quickly complicated by the visual power of women whose hair has fallen out and is now carried in red paper bags. Other women in white gowns scream as they carry more skulls across the stage.

Daughter of a black man and a white woman, daughter of a man and a woman, Sarah embodies not only the elemental tensions between these oppositions, but the conflicting social values attached to black and white, male and female. *Funnyhouse of a Negro* is not an examination of a woman's idiosyncratic, unique dissolution into madness but is an enacted metaphor – a genuine dramatisation – of cultural structures that make self-deceit and mendacity viable alternatives to self-hatred for a person who is black and female. Kennedy has spoken publicly about her admiration for the work of Tennessee Williams, and that influence is apparent in her emphasis, like his, on the destructive power of the lie. It is not, however, just the theatrical evidence of the corruption of lying in general that

111

empowers her dramaturgy. Her exposure of the usually protected wounds of black women haunts the spectator long after witnessing a performance.

Theatrical metaphors for those vulnerabilities became even more vivid in the six short plays Kennedy wrote in a burst of energy that followed the success of *Funnyhouse of a Negro*. The black brother and sister who are the central characters in *A Rat's Mass* each appear on stage as creatures who are caught in the moment of transformation from human being to rat; a procession that includes Jesus, Mary, Joseph, two wise men and a shepherd weaves in and out of Sister and Brother Rats' dialogue, catalysing the metamorphosis. The processional serves as choral witness to the siblings' recollections of their own incest, commanded by a white girl with worms in her hair. Women's greater vulnerability to sexual manipulation is made clear near the end of the play in the revelation that Sister Rat went mad after becoming pregnant by her brother and was sent to the State Hospital.

Still another Kennedy mini-play, *A Lesson in Dead Language*, suggests that there is no solace or support for the black woman in organised religion nor in other public institutions. Seven female adolescents dressed in white organdie are taught by a large white dog to repeat 'I bleed.' To become a woman, they learn, is to bleed and that in turn is to be 'a pinnacle tumbled down'. In the last image of this play, the girls stand before us, heads hanging down, their skirts covered with the blood that every adolescent girl fears will one day humiliate her.

A similar inclusion of the grotesque within a feminist critique of social institutions is present in the plays of Rochelle Owens. Here, too, bizarre images, usually drawn from the material of sexuality, defeat any stereotyped presumptions of what a feminine dramaturgy might be like.

1 Rita Tushingham as Nancy and Julian Glover as Tolen in *The Knack* by
Ann Jellicoe, London, 1962.

2   Rita Tushingham and Philip Locke in *The Knack*, London, 1962.

3   The Omaha Magic Theatre production of *Goona Goona* by Megan Terry with Jo Ann Schmidman and Gwen Andrews, 1979.

4   A 1979 production of *Vinegar Tom* by Caryl Churchill with Hilary Nelson, Jim Emery, Debbie Flics, Bob Hannum, Cheryl Stewart, Wendy Sax and Joyce Davis, at the Smith College Theatre Department, Northampton.

5   *Steaming* by Nell Dunn. *Left to right:* Georgina Hale as Josie, Ann Lynn as Nancy, Brenda Blethyn as Dawn, Patti Love as Jane, Maria Charles as Mrs Meadow and Jo Warne as Violet, at the Theatre Royal, Stratford, 1981.

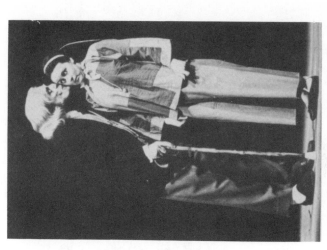

6 Carmen du Sautoy and Jane Lapotaire in *Piaf* by Pam Gems, at The Other Place, RSC, Stratford, 1981.

7 John Boswall as Mr Emanuelli and Jane Carr as Mary Mooney in *Once a Catholic* by Mary O'Malley, at the Royal Court Theatre, 1977.

8 *Crimes of the Heart* by Beth Henley. *Left to right:* Lee Anne Fahey, Kathy Bates, Susan Kingsley, at the Actors Theatre of Louisville, 1979.

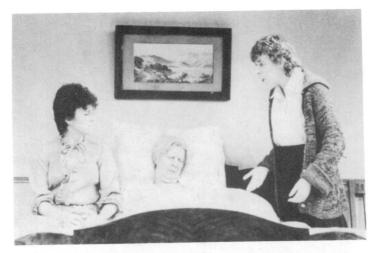

9 *Skirmishes* by Catherine Hayes at the Hampstead Theatre, 1982. *Left to right:* Gwen Taylor as Rita, Anna Wing as Mother and Frances de la Tour as Jean.

11 Susan Kingsley and Lynn Cohen in *Getting Out* by Marsha Norman, Actors Theatre of Louisville, 1977.

10 The New York Shakespeare Festival Production for Public Theatre in October 1976 of *for colored girls . . .* by Ntozake Shange, directed by Oz Scott, and produced by Joseph Papp. *Front to back:* Aku Kadogo, Rise Collins, Lawrie Carlos and Seret Scott.

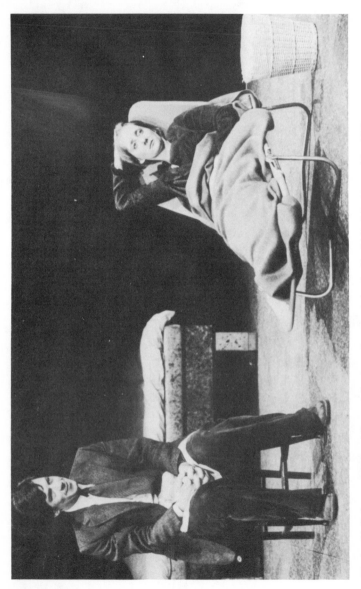

12 Ian McKellen as Colin and Gemma Jones as Anne in *Ashes* by David Rudkin, Young Vic, 1975.

Often set in ostensibly non-Western contexts – *Istanboul* takes place in the city of that name and *Beclch* focuses on a white green somewhere in Africa – Owens's dramas are all ultimately situated in the unspoken fantasies that occur between our sleeping and waking, our terrors and desires.

Of the more than twenty plays by Rochelle Owens that have been produced in theatres all over the world in the past twenty years, her Obie-award-winning *Futz* remains the best-known instance of what the drama critic Harold Clurman once called Owens's 'anthropology of fantasy'. The hero of the play, a candid, corn-fed farmer named Cy Futz, violates age-old rules of human behaviour by falling in love with, and making love with, his pig Amanda. A neighbour who witnesses Futz's passion for his sow is so intoxicated by the sight that he transforms his own heat into rage and murders a young woman. Futz is eventually blamed and jailed as the source of violence and upheaval in the community. His defence is that his neighbours came looking for the perversion they wanted to see: 'I wasn' near people!' he tells the prison warden. 'They came to me and looked under my trousers all the way up to their dirty hearts! They minded my own life.'[4]

But *Futz* is not just about the dirt in men's souls that they pretend is outside themselves, nor is its strategy simply an attempt to shock audiences through the exposure of eccentric sexual behaviour. Owens is what Wallace Stevens once called a 'metaphysician in the dark'; she leads us through the mysteries of the intangible and through mazes lined with questions that have no certain answers. Her medium is language and often her motif is sexuality, but almost always her interest is in what is enigmatic and surprising. In *Futz*, *Beclch* and *Istanboul*, as well as in Owens's more recent dramas, we encounter an embodiment of what Antonin Artaud meant by the theatre of

113

cruelty, a theatre in which the language is that of dreams, and erotic obsessions, where a utopian sense of life and 'even . . . cannibalism' constitute the illusion. Similar to many black playwrights of the sixties and seventies, Owens's language is often scatological; as in black drama, the violence of the dialogue correlates with the violence and the eroticism she perceives in human behaviour.

Istanboul begins with two fifteenth-century men watching a male Byzantine dancer. The first line of the play comments on the performance: 'He could ram my wife in the armpit!' Within seconds the conversation has moved on to the scales that replace a eunuch's cock, to buggering, and the beating of women to keep them faithful. Two Byzantine women participate without embarrassment in the conversation, and it is they, not the men, who start a physical fight. In the second scene of *Istanboul*, the wives of the two men from Scene one gossip, but in contrast to more stereotyped 'women's talk', Alice and Gertrude speak neither in euphemisms nor in code. They discuss the relative appeal of hairy women to both men and women, and they laugh at the naïve commercial schemes of their men. Only when Leo, the dancer, arrives to make love with Alice does her language change to the clichés usually put in the mouths of female characters.

Owens felt 'violated' by the weak first production of *Istanboul*, which was neither as wild nor as cross-culturally evocative as she had wished. Rather than reorienting the spectator to a microcosm in which Eastern and Western cultures met and crossed paths, the production was confusing and attempted to appeal facilely to a sense of the 'exotic'. The acting was unconvincing, and staging obviously symbolic rather than hypnotic or disturbing. It was in part a desire to achieve sympathetic productions of

114

her plays that led her to join the Women's Theater Council in 1972. Wit and farce are key tools in her craft, but both directors and reviewers have often missed the humour that accompanies the knife in the hands of feminist playwrights. Rochelle Owens's plays are too perplexing to be dismissed as didactic, the common accusation thrust at feminist dramas, but they also demand our tolerance of behaviour often considered deviant.

A parallel dramaturgical approach is evident in the plays of Julie Bovasso, a woman of labyrinthian theatrical achievements. Winner of five Obie awards in three different areas – best actress in 1955 for her role in Genet's *The Maids*; best experimental theatre award in 1955 for her Tempo Theater; and best actress, director *and* playwright for her many roles in *Gloria and Esperanza* in 1969 – Bovasso is a consummate theatre artist whose relative lack of public recognition is especially perplexing.

Despite Bovasso's multiple contributions, *Gloria and Esperanza* is not a one-woman show. Where Owens roams the universe from play to play, Bovasso takes us with her on an epic journey from underground hip culture of the sixties to the fantasy worlds of one of her central characters, the poet Julius Esperanza. A large cast of men and women play an even larger set of characters, transforming as they go from guru children to gladiators, from saints and martyrs to an eight-foot chicken and a cocker spaniel. Holding this zanily montaged world together is Gloria B. Gilbert (the role first played by Bovasso herself), girlfriend to the poet Julius Esperanza and pragmatist supreme. Gloria's ability to manipulate others is matched by her awesome rationality and relieved by her ability to make us laugh. Her ancestor is Ann in George Bernard Shaw's *Man and Superman*, a play that echoes throughout *Gloria and*

Esperanza. In contrast, however, to Shaw's Ann, whose last words to her husband are 'Never mind dear. Go on talking', Gloria's last spoken line is 'Kiss my ass.'

Rosalyn Drexler, yet another founder of the Women's Theater Council, writes with an equally caustic and unconventional prose which she has repeatedly applied to both fiction and drama. She, too, won an Obie award – for *Home Movies* in 1964 – but she had been writing for more than fifteen years before she received that recognition, and, even then, it was mainly through the support of other women, including Ellen Stewart at Café La Mama, that she was able to get solid productions of her plays.

Drexler, like Owens, attacks the treatment of women as objects and property, but whereas Owens's and Bovasso's women are often as remote and dissembling as are their male characters, Drexler's female characters are more frequently engaging models of a newly released strength or whimsical mouthpieces of women's wit. A widow with metaphysical powers, her nudist daughter and a nun in the process of 'breaking the habit', present wild, comic and evocative images of non-stereotyped women in *Home Movies*. Queen Hatshepsut, the historical heroine of a later Drexler play, *She Who Was He*, endures an exemplary struggle with a male power system that reveals both the seductions of authority and the distinctive understandings women have of sexuality, friendship and community.

Skywriting, one of Drexler's most frequently produced plays, captures the projections of self and other that form the basis of male–female interaction. In the simple plot, a woman and a man struggle over a postcard which we only see as a slide projection. The woman remembers that the window sills have to be dusted; the man obsessively tries to recall Keats's 'Ode to a Grecian Urn'. The man never escapes his own initial projections, but, in the world of this play, the woman understands the structure of power and property relations, names it and vows to alter it:

> WOMAN: You want it because it's mine. . . . And you think that I belong to you too, and that's why you want me. You want me and my art reproduction. You want my art reproduction and my entire reproduction system. You hate both my systems. The HOW TO LIVE FOREVER System and the HOW TO LIVE HARMONIOUSLY AS A WOMAN system.[5]

More starkly and unremittingly here than in some feminist dramas, man is the enemy. Implicitly, at least, Drexler's main audience is women; if her play works her audience will cheer the Woman's promise to surprise and conquer, and we will see the Man as foe to that attempt. In most of her other plays, Drexler tempers anger and opposition with a cacophonous mixture of puns, songs, verbal and visual transformations. But whether she parodies male lives as in Charlie the stuttering intellectual in *Home Movies*, or sketches male characters in a minimalist manner as she does with the Man in *Skywriting*, Drexler consistently unmasks the dangers in 'typical' aspects of male and female behaviour. Such dramaturgy allows no comfortable space for men in the audience but, although less extensively explored than in Caryl Churchill's plays, Drexler's dramas provoke us to re-examine gender roles and the arbitrary lines we draw between the sexes.

Maureen Duffy's *Rites*, first performed in the experimental programme of the National Theatre in London in 1969, further pursues antagonism between men and women. One of the first overtly feminist plays to be produced in Britain, *Rites*'s chorus of women gathered in a ladies' lavatory prefigures *Steaming*, Nell Dunn's success-

ful West End drama of a decade later. At the same time,
except for particularities of diction and accoutrements
uniquely characteristic of public lavatories in London, *Rites*
meshes with the network of feminist plays emerging during
the late sixties and early seventies in the United States.

Although five of the twelve women in the cast of *Rites*
have personal names, both the play itself and Duffy's
introduction to it emphasise the roots of the ensemble in
the chorus of Greek tragedy. Even more specifically, *Rites*
deliberately recalls the chorus of women in Euripides' *The
Bacchae*. The 'rites' referred to in the play's title include the
purging, washing up, combing and making-up that occur in
women's washrooms. In this case, the habitual nature of
these activities is made emphatic by the constant presence
of Ada, the lavatory's attendant. The women who use these
facilities, or ones just like them, appear there every day.
There is also a ritualised ambience to the conversation: the
protests of the office girls against the grafitti on the walls of
the cubicles have all been spoken before, as have the
complaints of the women about the monotony of their work
and the domination of their lives by men.

The difference on the day on which *Rites* takes place is
that Norma, one of the women who enters the washroom,
has secretly decided to put an end to all rites except the last.
Resuscitated and bandaged by her 'sisters', Norma survives
to reveal that her suicide attempt was provoked by a man's
abuse. Ada, Euripides' Agave metamorphosised into the
matron of the lavatory, erupts at this revelation: 'Bastard
men! Get a man she says. I'll get him right where I want
him.' That is precisely what the women do, or think they do.
Ada's explosion is contagious and provokes the other
women first to cry out their own rejections of men and then
to dance together, singing out 'We don't need them. Don't
need them.' In their frenzy, like the ancient Bacchae, the

women menace a short-haired, bent figure in coat and suit who hurriedly moves from another cubicle to the exit door. Mistaking the figure for a 'bloody man' who has been spying on the women in their one private space, they beat the person to death, then discover that their victim is a woman. Weak in their confusion, the chorus of women obey Ada's instruction to throw the body down the incinerator and to accept the shared guilt for the murder. Abruptly, the play ends with business as usual.

Were *Rites* to have ended with the women's choral rejection of men, the challenge to the audience would have been simpler and more easily dismissable. Instead, Duffy demands that we confront complexities at least as puzzling as those with which Euripides presented his audience. It is possible for both men and women to respect the anger of the play's women at men but it is equally important, Duffy suggests, that everyone confronts the distortion of vision that accompanies such fury. Murder is no answer, but, beyond that, male and female are not so easily distinguishable, one from the other. The deeper, more significant cause of fury in women may not be men but a profound sense of powerlessness.

Rites attempts to move women, and men too, away from easy slogans and self-righteous separatism, while simultaneously achieving a respect for communities of women and their need to escape victimisation. Similar attempts appear in a number of feminist plays of the early seventies, including Tina Howe's *Birth and After Birth* and Honor Moore's *Mourning Pictures*.

Howe and Moore had begun their own theatre networking in 1970 when Moore had co-produced Howe's play *The Nest* which, in turn, had played within blocks and weeks of the Public Theater's production of Myrna Lamb's *Mod Donna*.[6] Howe and Moore both recognise the theatrical

119

and political implications for women of rituals associated especially with life-cycles. The rite in Howe's *Birth and After Birth* is the birthday party of a four-year-old boy, played by an adult actor. Moore's *Mourning Pictures* pivots around the dying and death of Maggie, as perceived by her poet–daughter Margaret. In both plays, the transformation of the personal into the political shimmers just beneath the surface of the script, and, in both plays, vulnerability is hauntingly captured in the central female characters.

Glancing in a mirror after one of her son's tantrums, Sandy in *Birth and After Birth* quietly declares 'When I looked in the mirror this morning, I saw an old lady. Not *old* old, just used up.'[7] Margaret, in Moore's *Mourning Pictures* is stronger and more autonomous than Sandy, but in the moments where she reveals her own fragility, her dramatic power is most acute. Late one night, she leaves her dying mother's room, closing the door softly behind her:

> Halfway down the
> stairs I stop and put the dishes down,
> sit there and remember
> as hard as I can where I am, hard as
> I can: I am myself, a woman,
> nursing a woman who may be dying.
> My mother can't feed me any more.[8]

Neither Sandy nor Margaret is a model of virtue; what makes each exemplary is her attempt to confront her shame. Adrienne Kennedy's adolescent women, perhaps because they are black as well as female, are unable to transcend their shame and survive their wounds. For Moore's Margaret, however, the defeat and loss in her mother's death is accompanied by the knowledge that while 'the cheek flesh falls thin from the bones . . . she is not cold'.

Missing in most of the stage worlds created by this first network of feminist playwrights is the recognition of women by women. This is not a dramaturgical flaw, but it is a notable omission. The mother and daughter in *Mourning Pictures* are no more able to acknowledge each other than the two sisters in Churchill's *Top Girls*. For many women creating theatre in the late sixties and early seventies, authentic reflections of women had to reveal the hesitations women had in making themselves vulnerable with each other.

Of all the women engaged in the new network, it was Maria Irene Fornes who most systematically articulated this obstacle and tried to overcome it. Born in Cuba in 1930, Fornes was initially a painter. She immigrated to the United States in 1945, but it was not until the 1960s that she began to write plays, many of which were performed in the same off-Broadway contexts as were those of her sister playwrights. The Judson Poets' Theatre, the Open Theatre and eventually her own Promenade Theatre supported her work. A key figure in the founding of the Women's Theatre Council, when that group floundered in 1973 Fornes became president of its offspring, Theatre Strategy, an organisation of playwrights dedicated to sending experimental plays across the country 'the way one sends an army'. Ten years after she began to organise that army, its victories would be ironically articulated by Marsha Norman, Pulitzer-prize-winning author of the 1983 Broadway success *'night, Mother.* Apparently unaware of her precursor's words, Norman described her fellow playwrights as 'this battalion, marching valiant soldiers on the front lines'. Getting that army to the front line was the work that Maria Irene Fornes undertook.

Although her administrative efforts were effective, it is in Fornes's fifteen or more plays that we still see the best evidence of the theatrical weapons she deploys in the service of feminism. 'Masculine rivalry' motivates much of the conflict in one of her early plays, *The Successful Life of Three*, in which a character identified only as 'He' and another identified as '3' transform through stages of their lives but consistently treat the character named 'She' as an object or servant. 'She' is ostensibly the stereotype of the dumb, sexy woman, yet, with each new stage in her life, 'she' changes most and insistently disturbs the assumptions of her male partners about female behaviour. A play that rests almost entirely on stark, rapid dialogue, what emerges in *The Successful Life of Three* is Fornes's special combination of comic exaggeration with what she has called a 'tenderness' for her characters.

That tenderness becomes more intense and structured in each of Fornes's subsequent plays. *Molly's Dream*, first presented in 1968, is at once a parody of romantic saloon scenes from film and theatre and a constructive projection of women in rebellion against the traditional dynamics of romantic love. Molly, the heroine of the play, is a barroom waitress who at first is a classical female victim of love for a man who abuses her. Although structurally separated from them, she is thematically one of the play's chorus of 'Hanging Women' who cling to the men they adore. Molly, however, decides not to remain a victim, and we see her struggle through various stages of her growth, stages she herself recognises as necessary by the end of the play. Through Molly's developing strength, the Hanging Women also change, as they tell us in a series of songs that eventually reject the 'old, old withered idea, without reward' of true love. *Molly's Dream* dismisses neither men nor love, but demands instead that men and women 'become what we are'. The uncertainty at the end of the play, as voiced by Molly herself, is whether or not the man she once loved will recognise her when she fully becomes herself.

Fornes's best-known play, *Fefu and Her Friends*, begun in the early seventies and first produced in New York in 1977 by Theater Strategy, structurally and thematically extends this concern with the relationship between transformation and recognition. The entire cast is now a chorus of women, a group of eight who come together in Fefu's house to plan an unspecified educational project. Early in the play, Fefu declares to one of her guests that she still likes men better than women in part because 'they are well together. Women are not.' Fefu's attention focuses on women, but she disconcerts her female friends with her ambivalent behaviour towards men and her admission that she has not yet learned how to conquer her own submission to them. She will not allow herself or others to deny the roles they play, as is evident from her opening line: 'My husband married me to have a constant reminder of how loathsome women are.'

More than her friends, Fefu struggles with the difficulty of the battle for women with women:

> Women have to find their natural strength and when they do find it, it comes forth with bitterness and it's erratic. . . . Women are restless with each other. They are like live wires . . . either chattering to keep themselves from making contact or else, if they don't chatter, they avert their eyes like Orpheus . . . as if a god once said 'and if they shall recognize each other, the world will be blown apart . . .'[9]

Fornes's goal is not the traditional self-recognition of one character, but a collective and mutual acknowledgement of women by other women, as individuals and members of a group. To turn the audience towards this, Fornes attempts the unusual strategy of moving the audience from one space to another during the performance. We watch the opening scene from spectator seats facing a stage. For the central portion of the performance, however, we are asked to move, in four groups, around the 'house', to the lawn, the study, the bedroom and the kitchen. In each environment, two or three of the characters are encountering each other; we witness, then move on to another room as the actresses repeat the scene for the next group. At the end of the play, all characters return to the living room and we to our places in the auditorium.

With this movement of the audience from space to space, Fornes engages the spectator in the environment, reinvoking Gertrude Stein's notion of drama as landscape. In almost all of the plays discussed in this chapter, environment plays a key role, but with this movement of the audience in *Fefu* Fornes has brought that element forward, much as Megan Terry and Caryl Churchill have made transformation an overt rather than covert theatrical convention. This manipulation of the audience obviously alters the relationship of spectator to performer, establishing intimacy and a necessity for a distinct performance style. Fornes, who directed *Fefu* herself, speaks of this style as cinematic. In addition, the activity of the audience places greater responsibility on us – by moving from scene to scene we *follow* the drama and are less passive recipients of it.

At the end of *Fefu and Her Friends* the world is not blown apart, but one shot is heard that resounds as a premonition of the future. Haunting Fefu and the other women throughout the play has been the troubling figure of Julia, imprisoned in a wheel chair to which she has been confined – or confined herself – since a strange hunting accident in which she symbolically suffered the pain of a slaughtered deer. Julia's terror – of violence, of men and of her own visions – has made her apparently insane. She lives the opposite side of Fefu's paradox; as aware as Fefu of the enormity of the struggle women must undertake, Julia chooses not to fight but to yield. Fefu, however, will not let Julia go. Unable to reinvigorate her friend verbally, Fefu moves to Julia's symbolic terrain and shoots a rabbit whose blood then appears on Julia's forehead. The lights fade as the remaining six women move to the stage and surround Julia. Symbolically at least, and on stage where all things are possible, the woman-as-victim must be killed in her own terms in order to ignite the explosion of a community of women.

6
Communities of Women in Drama: Pam Gems, Michelene Wandor, Ntozake Shange

By the mid-1970s, the women's movement in both Britain and the United States was no longer the isolated terrain of scattered groups of women dismissable as eccentric, unfeminine or academic. Although never fully organised nationally in either country, it became a mass movement with vast legal and social ramifications, a movement that provoked aggressive assaults from its increasingly visible opposition and that suffered internal conflicts concerning values and future strategies. Consciousness-raising groups, a main source of energy in the late sixties and early seventies, were gradually vanishing from the scene, and public media and institutions were making modest if often hollow gestures towards 'equality' of the sexes. In the United States, women spoke of 'radical feminism', a conceptualisation of society and power in which men and women were oppositional forces, and in which a patriarchical tradition had to be overthrown; a number of women turned to psychoanalytical techniques to examine personal and collective issues of identity and power. In Britain, a

126

socialist–feminism emerged that placed its emphasis on a conjoining of gender analysis with class analysis; here, the methodology was a modification of Marxism in which women's economic and social liberation would instigate rather than follow structural changes in society.

Like the early stage of the contemporary women's movement itself, the outburst of feminist plays and playwrights discussed in the previous chapter took consciousness-raising as one of its primary goals. Parodies of stereotypes of women, role reversals, vivid imagings of female sexuality and women's ambivalences about their bodies were all non-reductive strategies intended to make women and men more aware of their gender-related behaviour and attitudes. Megan Terry and Caryl Churchill were already exploring alternative dramatic strategies in the early seventies: both were re-examining history through theatre, and both were extending the implications of transformations by challenging perceptions of rigid distinctions between men and women. Almost all of the playwrights whose work became public in the sixties and early seventies have continued to write. Their plays are produced in regional theatres around the world, in alternative theatres in London, off-off Broadway and occasionally at the Public Theater in New York, but yet remain relatively unknown.

Still somewhat hidden in the forest of male-dominated theatre, the first wave of feminist drama had created a clearing, and, by the mid-seventies, a number of other feminist dramatists were building solid structures on that land. Dozens of plays were produced in Britain and the United States, written by individuals and collectives whose primary intent was to let the voices of women be heard. Susan Griffin's *Voices*, Viveca Lanfors, *I Am Woman*, Eve Merriam's *Out of Our Father's House* were three among many feminist plays that attempted what playwright–director Karen Malpede has called 'breaking the silence which keeps us complicit in our own destruction'. In many instances, this took the form of calling forth the voices of women from the past, women who these playwrights felt had been unfairly silenced in their time.

Surrounded by the strength of these 'voices', three women playwrights especially focused their attention on a theatrical vision of women in community. Two of these – Pam Gems and Michelene Wandor – began working with experimental theatre groups in London in the early seventies and gradually came to public attention in the late 1970s as major figures in feminist drama. The third, the black American woman Ntozake Shange, worked her way and her play *for colored girls who have considered suicide when the rainbow is enuf* from a café in San Francisco to the shining lights of Broadway. Thematically, these three playwrights shared many concerns: women and work, children, class and gender, women's history and women's fortitude are important in all of their plays. Each of these women also continued earlier attempts to explore alternatives to bourgeois realism. The most remarkable continuity in the plays of Gems, Wandor and Shange is not in their shared motifs or experimental energy, but in their ability to move beyond autonomy and the melodies of single voices to the explosive sounds of women talking and singing with each other.

Pam Gems, the oldest of these three playwrights, was heralded as a 'major' playwright in 1980 when *Piaf*, her musical dramatisation of the life of Edith Piaf, achieved commercial success on the West End and Broadway. Gems had been writing radio and television scripts since the 1950s, and had already written or adapted eleven other produced stage dramas in the seventies before *Piaf* (actually written some years before) became a hit. Born in rural England in 1925, her personal history is notably similar to that of Caryl Churchill. Like Churchill, Gems married immediately after completing university studies and reared four children while writing radio and television plays at home. In the early seventies, her children were growing into adulthood, new opportunities for experimental theatre were opening in London, and the women's liberation movement was gaining momentum and Gems's attention. She moved to London and became immersed in fringe productions with feminist orientations.

Although she has rejected the label 'feminist playwright',[1] Gems's plays and her statements about theatre have consistently articulated a strong feminist vision. Comparison of her versions of *Uncle Vanya* and *A Doll's House* with other translations, for example, reveals her keen eye for the subtle disturbances and internal turmoil of women struggling with dual roles. She speaks honestly of the difficulty for women playwrights of having a family and the kind of total commitment necessary to write. And she speaks harshly of the 'connections' necessary to get plays produced, ties made in contexts usually closed to women. Yet in a voice that echoes Gertrude Stein, she is optimistic about the prospects for feminist drama:

Art is of necessity. Which is why we need women playwrights just now very badly. We have our own history to create, and to write. Personally, I think there will be brilliant women playwrights. I think the form suits us. Women are very funny, coarse, subversive. All good qualities for drama, and for the achievement of progress by the deployment, not of violence, but of subtlety, love, imagination.[2]

The qualities Gems commends in women are abundant in her own writing and in the characters she creates. Many of her plays focus on complicated historical or mythical women – Queen Christina, Rosa Luxemburg, Guinevere, Piaf – for whom public roles conflict with prior desires. Her Piaf *is* very funny and coarse, and in emphasising those characteristics rather than taking a more soothing, romanticised version of the famous French songstress, Gems achieved a subversion both of female stereotype and theatrical expectations. Piaf, as performed in both London and the United States by Jane Lapotaire, is never conventionally beautiful, nor is she the cute little sparrow her name might suggest. She is a constant paradox – strong but fragile, generous and needy, coarse yet elegant. The play stays in the memory as a one-woman show, yet in actuality the script and production have a large cast of characters who continually move in and around the lonely star.

London critics praised *Piaf* while New York critics damned it and often on the same grounds. The script is deliberately episodic and calls for constant transformations of place, time and relationships. Ordered in a rough chronology, each scene reveals a historical context that adds a fragment to a picture of a whole life. Despite the chronology, the whole is more a collage than a montage; with each new episode Piaf's life becomes more complex but it does not move towards recognition, reversal or resolution. With the exception of Toine, a woman friend from the same working-class background as Edith Piaf, others, especially men, make brief, sharp cuts in the fabric of Piaf's life, then vanish, leaving the tear and no material substance. Critics who disliked the play found this parade of characters unsatisfying. They were also disappointed by Gems's decision to use few of Piaf's best-known songs among the nine performed in the show.

Many of these dramaturgical choices are familiar in the context of feminist theatre, and, in that context, can be seen as deliberate political decisions. Gems's Piaf retains her working-class mores including language habits throughout her life and the show, but to do so in the context of her stardom, her success and her female identity is difficult and disorienting – for use and for Piaf herself. The moment when Piaf lifts her skirt and pisses on stage is at once an aggressive and liberating gesture to the audience; it breaks the convention that no stage character ever urinates – except some recent 'oddities' like Beckett's Krapp – and reminds us of the euphemisms of the 'ladies' room'.

Piaf's friendship with Toine *is* the only sustained relationship presented. Whether or not this is true to the 'facts' of Piaf's life, it is credible within the life constructed on stage. Most people, and especially her male lovers, were unable to maintain intimacy with Piaf. If her music was harmonious, her life was cacophonous, and few people could endure either the lack of fulfilment of their own desires or Piaf's erratic needs for sex, drugs and solitude. Within this frame, Gems's decision to use a number of Piaf's less familiar songs can be seen as a deliberate attempt to keep the balance between the roughness of Piaf's life and the power of the music – too much nostalgia in the songs, too much nostalgia in the audience.

Although *Piaf* was not produced until 1978, it was a relatively early Gems play and the work that followed it, *Dusa, Fish, Stas and Vi*, elaborates many of Gems's dramatic strategies. Piaf's tiny community of two grows to a community of four women in *Dusa, Fish, Stas and Vi*, and here the failure of fruitful relationships with men is endemic, coded and social. Each of the women in the play is a type or even archetype, but each also resists stereotyping. Dusa has a talent for spatial design although she is not

131

working. She resembles 'a Vogue fashion model, off-duty'. Her main focus during the time of the play is the retrieval of her two children when her ex-husband has kidnapped. Fish is an elegant, upper-middle-class intellectual, an effective orator for a left-wing political group. Her attention is divided between a commitment to politics and an obsession with her ex-lover, Alan. Stas is the most overtly divided of the four women: during the day she is a physiotherapist trying to learn all she can about biology; at night she works as a high-class call-girl in order to save money to do graduate work in marine biology. Her background is rural working class; her father was a tenant farmer. Vi, the youngest of the four, is just out-growing adolescence. Her background is urban working-class, and, for most of the play, she defines herself by her anorexia; she is weak and high on amphetamines much of the time in the first part of the play.

The circumstances that bring these four women under the same roof are never explained. The unstated grounds of their relationships are a mutual acceptance that demands no explanation. To be genuinely in community, however, more than passive acceptance is necessary, and it is the ability − or inability − of each of the women to be responsible to the others that establishes the main tensions of the drama.

Vi, who never leaves the flat, grounds the household. Stas complements Vi: she consistently transforms the scene as she transforms herself from a 'plain, competent-looking girl in a white overall' and dowdy coat to a glamorous 'hostess', a creature of sumptuous and startling beauty'. Stas uses men, but like Vi and in contrast to Dusa and Fish, she does not allow her life to be affected by them. Throughout the play, Stas reminds her housemates and us of the real possibility of change and the resources of

132

personal commitment and exploitation of roles that can facilitate change. Gems has written about the influence of music on her dramaturgy in this play, and, as these women's lives interrupt, punctuate and support each other, a structure emerges similar to that of a jazz quartet. In this structure, it is Stas who provides the counter-melody, the disconcerting sounds and images that make us pay attention.

Music also serves to link the many scenes of the play, conceived as 'fragments' or movie 'takes'. This episodic, cinematic mode also functions like classical montage, producing what Sergei Eisenstein called 'the collision of images'. In isolation, each of these women's struggles would be poignant but flat; juxtaposed to each other, each woman's battle for strength and survival inspires the others and points to deep social structures that support patriarchy and woman's own weak self-image.

In contrast to Fornes's *Fefu and Her Friends*, Gems's world of women is neither transitory nor internally conflictual but a construct in which the spectator can invest hope and belief. Easy to overlook because it so permeates the dialogue, one of the most remarkable characteristics of *Dusa, Fish, Stas and Vi* is the attendance of the characters to each other's words and needs. Not one of these women is perfect in her generosity or recognition of the others, but they do learn and change from their failures. Not one of them is a model of the 'ideal' woman, but, importantly, the absence of deceit and manipulation among them serves as a model for how women might be together.

Given this positive construct, Fish's suicide at the end of the play shocks the audience and provoked controversy among spectators and reviewers. Because Fish is associated with left-wing politics, her death was unhappily viewed by some as a denigration of the left. Yet it is precisely because

Fish is unable to resolve the conflicts between her political theory and her personal inclination to subjugate herself to her lover that she suffers so intensely and finally kills that suffering and herself. Faced with the difficulty of being productive and reproductive, of being workers and mothers, of achieving and nurturing, each of the other women has narrowed her desires and commitments: Stas commits herself to her profession, Dusa to her children, Vi to her body. Fish is greedier than the rest, less willing to settle for what she sees as half a life. She recognises the pain as well as the productive passion in her heroine, Rosa Luxemburg, who 'never married Leo. She never had the child she longed for.' But Fish cannot accept those limits for herself.

Fish's suicide is tragic. It is not a cynical or defeatist gesture but a powerful reminder to the audience of the limitations of individual effort and the insufficiency of the liberation of women as a separatist endeavour. Fish tries to change herself, but she cannot overcome the mental structures of class and gender in which she was raised. She inspires the other women, Vi especially, to fight for control over their lives, but she is defeated by the apparent incompatibility of love and autonomy. Fish's death calls attention to the central paradox of the play: removed from the company of men, women can focus fruitfully on women, but like the perfectly enclosed worlds of theatre, communities of women exist in a larger society that obviously includes men. *Dusa, Fish, Stas and Vi* argues forcefully that recognition of women by women is a crucial step in overcoming oppression. It foresees the next step – re-creation of men's and women's relationships to each other – as more difficult than any change yet attempted. The final words of the play and of Fish's suicide note cry to other women for help: 'My loves, what are we to do? We won't do as they want anymore, and they hate it. What are we to do?'³

A number of responses have come to that plea since Gems wrote *Dusa* in 1975. Important among them is the voice of poet–playwright–critic Michelene Wandor. Wandor had worked in theatre in the early stages of her career, and in 1969 began writing plays to combine her interests in poetry and performance. By 1971, she was Poetry Editor and a regular theatre-reviewer for *Time Out* magazine in London and had also become heavily involved in the early stages of the women's liberation movement. Her first produced play, *The Day After Yesterday*, lambasted the sexual hypocrisy in the 'Miss World' contest. Its presentation in 1972, followed by *Spilt Milk* and *To Die Among Friends*, contributed significantly to the beginnings of feminist theatre in Britain.

A graduate of Cambridge University, and the daughter of working-class *émigrés* from the Soviet Union, Wandor brings to both her creative and historical writings a profound class-consciousness and a sophisticated education from an institution that has consistently fertilised the work of experimental theatre artists. She identifies her perspective with that of Pam Gems, but her position is more accurately described as at the fulcrum of socialist–feminist–gay theatre. *Understudies*, her historical account of theatre and sexual politics in Britain in the seventies, and her two anthologies of plays dealing with sexual politics, *Plays by Women* and *Strike While the Iron is Hot*, bring feminist drama to public attention. More than any single figure, Wandor is responsible for articulating and supporting the interaction of feminism, theatre, socialism and gay liberation in Britain.

Wandor's nine dramas focus on major feminist issues – women and work, caring for children, custody, divorce, lesbianism – explored through a variety of forms and modes of production. Diverging somewhat from other feminist playwrights, she has asserted a political commitment to realism, based on the historical understanding that 'artistic movements which seek to represent the experiences of oppressed groups reach initially for a realistic and immediately recognisable clarity'.[4] For her this calls for the grounding of plays in everyday activities. Her attempt is to 'break through the boundaries of naturalistic storytelling' while drawing on the authentic material of women's lives.

The tie to realism is strongest and most apparent in *Care and Control* written in 1977 in collaboration with the experimental theatre company Gay Sweatshop. Following performances of Gay Sweatshop's first feminist production, Jill Posener's *Any Woman Can*, the company asked audience members for topics for other plays. A repeated suggestion was 'the problems facing lesbian mothers in custody cases'.[5] The company conducted interviews and research on this issue, but then called in Wandor to do the actual script. As a single parent with 'care and control' of her child, Wandor brought personal and professional experience to the process. She worked closely with the company on the script, which drew heavily on actual cases, and the play opened in May 1977.

The first act of *Care and Control* moves back and forth among episodes in the lives of four couples: two of the couples – Sara and Stephen, Elizabeth and Gerald – are struggling with unhappy marriages; a third couple, Carol and Sue, are also near the ends of heterosexual marriages although we never see their male mates; Elizabeth and her lover, Chris, are an emerging couple. The intermingled and juxtaposed complexity of these relationships anticipates Caryl Churchill's *Cloud Nine*, but the presentation here is straightforward and serious with none of the satiric humour present in Churchill's sexual pot-pourri. The function of the multiple stories is much like that of a classical multiple-plot drama: being a parent and post-divorce custody of children are the common elements in each plot, and the specific variations in each relationship reveal an actual and an ideal hierarchy of values.

Care and Control is a morality play with two clear messages for the audience: it must challenge those who are socially empowered and use their roles to uphold the heterosexual, nuclear family above many other human values, and it must fight to assure that women are treated as full and equal human beings. The force of the play lies in its ability to effect this instruction dramatically. *Care and Control* does not preach at the spectator; rather, gently but insistently, it builds a set of situations that inspire our anger by showing the emotional and physical violence of men towards women. Both Stephen and Gerald are blind to the needs of their wives and children; neither man partakes in the raising of his child but both assert their proprietary rights to the children once the marriages are dissolved. The slides we are intermittently shown of each of the mothers giving birth and caring for her children remind us of the daily investment of women in being parents. The male characters ignore these images.

The particular slices of life Wandor chooses are certainly not exhaustive and could be criticised for their consistently positive presentations of women and negative depictions of men. Act II of *Care and Control*, however, makes the point that whether or not there are substantial numbers of exceptions to these characterisations of men and women, society supports patriarchical values and structures and disparages feminism and lesbianism. 'Society' is represented by a series of voices of 'authority', played, significantly, by each of the women in the cast as well as by one

137

male actor. This non-naturalistic convention is essential for it emphasises the transcendence of structure and roles over individual character or gender: placed in a role of institutional authority, even women we have come to know and respect will undermine other women. Chris plays the role of the judge who grants custody to Sara's ex-husband because he has remarried; later, Sara is the judge who determines that Elizabeth's 'feminist fanaticism' will be a bad influence on her son and thus her husband should have custody. That it is a male judge who actually grants custody to Carol is hardly a triumph of liberation in the context of the judge's 'conditions' that Carol and Sue keep their lesbian relationship private even inside their own house.

Most of Wandor's plays that follow *Care and Control* take a similar hard look at conventionalised or institutionalised biases against women. Increasingly, however, she has experimented with comedy and with presentational modes. The title of her next play, *Whores D'Oeuvres*, is whimsical and its setting is surrealistic: two prostitutes find themselves on a makeshift raft on the Thames after a freak hurricane. Along with their comical attempts to bolster each other's spirits, the two women, Tina and Pat, discuss their profession. Here, as in *Care and Control*, the audience is instructed throughout the play: in this instance, 'all women are prostitutes' and economic oppression is conjoined with sexual oppression as the cause of this condition. *Whores D'Oeuvres* resists its own didacticism by the inclusion of dream sequences that rhythmically interrupt the dialogue with dramatic verse, irreverent songs and exaggerated simulations of archetypal moments in the life of a whore.

The most striking exception among Wandor's plays to this tendency towards agit-prop is her full-length verse-drama *Aurora Leigh*. Based on Elizabeth Barrett Browning's epic poem of the same title, Wandor's dramatisation of Aurora's battles for autonomy and for recognition as a writer allows the playwright to let loose her own inclinations towards verse in a context where the verbal form matches the tale. Wandor paid particular attention to what she calls 'the clusters of "feminine" imagery', which in the play are Aurora's choices. According to the author, Aurora's poetry is also deliberately feminist in its strategy: 'Aurora is turning the passive nature imagery with which women have been objectified in men's love poetry into an active weapon as part of her struggle for autonomy.'[6]

Aurora finds autonomy, but she also takes the crucial next steps towards community with others. She is a genuine heroine, and the play is constructed upon her voice and presence so that we are led to applaud the triumph of individual autonomy. But Aurora is also a new kind of heroine. Because she is female, she is taught 'to be womanly' and given books on womanhood, 'To prove, if women do not think themselves, / They may teach thinking; books demonstrating / Their right of comprehending husband's talk / When not too deep.'[7] Romney, her cousin and great love, disparages her desire to write and tries to convince her that she would use her natural female talents better as his wife, assisting him in his work of touching 'life's victims'. Aurora resists these early lessons and temptations, but her commitment to her work is costly. Like Fish in Gems's *Dusa, Fish, Stas and Vi*, Aurora does not wish to sit alone and loveless, but, in contrast to Fish, she transcends her ambivalence and chooses for *her* life and *her* work.

Endurance and achievement of autonomy do not suffice to make her a special heroine. Alone in Paris, awaiting the sale of her book, she encounters Marion, to whom Romney had once been engaged. Marion, we discover, had been bribed and persuaded by one Lady Waldemar to reject Romney because she was not of his class. Raped and robbed shortly after her exodus to Paris, Marion is now a mother of a 'fatherless' son. Aurora needs Marion as much as Marion needs her, and although too sparsely presented, the love these two women discover for each other and for Marion's son strengthens them both. Nurturance from this relationship and from the success of her book finally allow Aurora to accept Romney's love for her and to admit a seachange: 'I write to live – yes; but live to live too.'

The end of the play is an alteration of Browning's poem in which a vanquished Romney, blinded in the fire that destroys his home, turns his life over to Aurora. Having depicted the steps a woman must take to achieve the kind of self-possession that would allow genuine partnership, Wandor concluded that to end with the domination of female over male was not progress but only an exchange of roles in the same intolerable structure. Her Romney thus returns to Aurora in full possession of his sight. Romney's and Aurora's reunion at the end of the play marks a rare instance in feminist drama of renewal and constructive change for both men and women.

Feminist dramas are characterised by the 'care and control' their authors give to language, as if the words on stage were the children of the writers' thoughts. Wandor goes further with *Aurora Leigh*, making the language the primary gesture of her drama, and the play a work that rests as easily on the page as on the stage. If there is a weakness to *Aurora Leigh* it is in the sufficiency of the words which suggest the pleasure but not the necessity of performance.

Almost the opposite is true of the most successful verse-drama by an American woman, Ntozake Shange's *for colored girls who have considered suicide when the rainbow is enuf.* Like Wandor, Shange is a poet and one who is committed to moving 'our theater into the drama of our lives'.[8] Shange, in fact, identifies herself as a poet '*in* American theater', and refuses to present herself as a playwright because of the sterility and irrelevance she perceives in most contemporary drama. Her rejection of the label 'playwright' is also, however, an objection to the usual notion that serious drama excludes dance and music; for Shange, any serious drama by a black playwright must include music and dance as equal partners in the activity, because singing and dancing are important 'cultural realities' for black people.

Shange's emphasis on music and dance as well as her poetic and political attempts to take the language 'apart to the bone'[9] are rooted in the black American experience but are also consistent with the inclinations of feminist drama. For Shange, as for Adrienne Kennedy, to be black and a woman are not antagonistic identities but are mutually reinforcing of both vulnerability and strength. Her tracing of her own history, in the introduction to *for colored girls*, attributes much of her inspiration and understanding of history to the women's movement as it entered her life through readings sponsored by feminist presses in California, the Woman's Studies programme at Sonoma State College in California, the Woman's Collective sponsorship of women poets and, finally, the collective she formed with four other women that became the core 'company' of *for colored girls*.

The first presentation by this company, at the Bacchanal, a woman's bar in Berkeley, California, was a raw sketch of what evolved into one of the longest-running productions in Broadway history. Consonant with the experience of so many women in the theatre, the five performers created the show, based initially on seven of Shange's poems, and also performed it. As one performance led to another, up and

141

down the California coast and then to New York, Shange worked with Paula Moss to unite their fragments of song, dance and poetry and create what they came to call a choreopoem.

From the beginning, Shange's motivating image was that of 'combat breathing' a concept that she borrowed from Franz Fanon and which has informed all her subsequent work. The term resonates to gender and class as well as racial conflict. Fanon's definition of 'combat breathing' is, in fact, explained in the context of culturally controlled 'landscapes': it is the necessary reaction of people whose territory is occupied. In Shange's terms, it is 'the living response / the drive to reconcile the irreconcilable'.

Whether in dance or song or poetry, or all three combined as is often the case in her theatre pieces, Shange's own 'combat breathing' is transformed again and again into stories, and most especially stories of and by women. Ming Cho Lee's set for *for colored girls* was bare of furniture and painted black. One huge hot-pink paper rose, hung on the upstage left wall, was the single blast in this otherwise stark landscape. It is a stage set *for* storytelling, not one, as in realistic drama, that tells a story itself.

Seven black women, the entire cast of *for colored girls*, begin the play by running onto the stage and freezing 'in postures of distress'.[10] Each performer is identified by a colour, and together these colours form a rainbow that therefore lacks both black and white. During the 90-minute performance, each of the women changes a number of times from character to chorus member and on to another character, retaining only the continuity of her own person and the colour she displays. The lady in brown speaks first, demanding of the women on-stage, and of the audience, that they allow a black girl to sing, that they acknowledge her song, that they 'let her be born'.[11]

142

As each of the other 'ladies' then announces herself, she does so by locating her origins in a place. That each of these women is from 'outside' one or another American city suggests both the marginality of the women and the continuity of their experiences with black women from all over the United States. The concept of theatrical land-scapes, latent in so many feminist dramas, here becomes manifest.

The stories we hear tell of epiphanic moments in the lives of black girls as they grow into womanhood. Each story contributes to a contained vision, not of a single character, but of a world that includes at the same time that it silences each of these voices. The lady in yellow grins as she recalls the loss of her virginity on 'graduation nite'. The lady in blue tells of the pretence she shared with her father that they were Puerto Rican, when in reality they 'waz just reglar niggahs wit hints of Spanish'.[12] The lady in red relates her devotion to a lover that lasted until she could no longer stand 'not being wanted when i wanted to be wanted'. Each of these stories is punctuated by songs and dance, per-formed by varying combinations of the entire cast who remain on stage to serve as witnesses and commentators in much the same manner that the chorus in Greek drama oversaw the main action. As all of the women dance following the first set of stories, they declare that they have 'come here to be dancin'.

The combination of the energetic joy in the women's dancing and the wit and self-mocking irony in their narrations makes it easy at first to overlook the pain that is also present from the very beginning of the play. In the next sequence of stories, however, where rape, abortion and humiliation are the topics, knowledge is paired with suffering and memory brings little pleasure. An irresistibly funny tale of a young girl's search for Toussaint L'Ouverture, the black Haitian hero whom she discovers in a library book, provides a brief reprise from the tension being built on stage.

As the play continues, without intermission, the series of anecdotes build an epic tale of the attempts of women to resist domination and dependency and the prices they pay in so doing. The lady in red, whose orange butterflies and aqua sequins inspired the play's title, narrates a story of a woman who took her vengeance on men for all women by making herself so seductive that she was a wound to every man arrogant enough to want her. She maintained control of her own life and her relationships to men, but each time she dismissed her evening's lover and 'finished writin the account of her exploit in a diary / embroidered with lilies & moonstones / she placed the rose behind her ear / and cried herself to sleep'.[13]

The dancing of the performers becomes increasingly intense and collective as *for colored girls* approaches its climax. The activity of listening to each other's stories draws the women to each other and transforms their individual shame, ironic distance and bitterness into communal anger and self-assertion. This sets up the context for the final, shocking story of the play, told by the woman in red about Crystal, her children and the children's father, Beau Willie. Crystal repeatedly rejects Beau Willie, a Vietnam war veteran, because he can only express his need for her through a violence that almost kills her. As the story nears its conclusion, we are caught between Beau Willie's despair and Crystal's need to protect herself and her children. In a last, desperate attempt to overcome Crystal's resistance, Beau Willie holds their children outside a window five storeys above ground and threatens to drop them unless Crystal publicly proclaims that she will marry him. The narration, presented initially in nervous rushes and bursts of recollected terror, ends quietly: 'i stood by beau in the window / with naomi rechin for me / and kwame screamin mommy mommy from the fifth story / but i cd only whisper / & he dropped em.'[14] In finishing her account, the woman who has been telling us *about* Crystal so fluidly shifts from 'she' to 'i' that the spectator takes a moment to comprehend the vulnerability – and the courage – displayed in this transformation.

For the women on-stage, the shared witnessing of Crystal's naked pain breaks any remaining barriers of isolation and introspection and brings about a gesture of mutual acknowledgement of each other as women with a common history. The women of all colours approach one another and lay their hands on each other out of necessity and desire. They are no longer able to sing or speak or dance alone.

It is no accident or weakness that *for colored girls*, in common with many feminist productions, has no 'lead' role and in performance resists the audience's expectation that one woman will emerge as a star or particular heroine. All of the performers are a chorus and each is also an individual. Even when Tarzana Beverly, a charismatic stage presence, performed the story of Crystal, her power surprised the audience because her presentation of self throughout the show was self-effacing and antithetical to stereotypes of star actresses. In the women's bars where *for colored girls* was born this would not be so unusual but such a gesture is noteworthy on Broadway.

Of Shange's recent work, *Boogie Woogie Landscapes*, presented initially as a one-woman piece in New York in 1978 and subsequently performed by a full cast, most vividly continues this aggressive experimentation with the conjoining of feminist and black aesthetics. In contrast to *for colored girls, Boogie Woogie Landscapes* reveals the visions and memories of one woman, but, again, there is a chorus, in this instance comprised of three women and three men who are the central character's 'night-life companions'.

The importance of landscape as a metaphor for her dramaturgy is once more asserted by Shange in the stage directions as well as the play's title. 'This is a geography,' the directions begin, 'of whimsy, fantasy, memory & the night.'[15] Layla, the protagonist, dances her way through the landscape of her life, finding partners from her history and her own prophecies. In the first half of the play she encounters aspects of her identity as a black person. She rejects even her own body because 'she did not want anything as black as the palms of her hands / to touch her', then learns and embraces the knowledge that 'there are horizons. there are different dawns' as close as in her own black hands.[16]

To be black and a woman, to be each of these, is to have two distinct mountains to climb, and having conquered one, layla (Shange consistently resists capitalisation of names) must as a woman begin to climb again. Everywhere, she sees women as victims, surrounded by the threat of rape, rejection, infibulation, genital excision, clitorectomy, and the constant fear of simply walking home alone at night. 'Such thoughts,' reflects one of the night-life companions, 'lead to a silence.' But the silence can be broken, as layla herself breaks it, through not one voice, but many that tell stories we cannot forget. The woman's body can dance and triumph over her victimisation, as it persistently does on stage in all of Shange's theatre pieces.

In theatre, such triumphs are momentary and the invitation to dance is often left unanswered. For Shange as was the case for Pam Gems, the commercial success of one play helped to secure production of subsequent work but did not ensure widespread applause. *for colored girls* met with mixed receptions among American blacks; in addition to those who praised the play, there were some who condemned its hostility towards men and others who felt Shange's bourgeois background misshapes her vision. Much as Gems's *Piaf* perplexed American audiences when it was brought from the West End to Broadway, *for colored girls* disappointed English spectators. With both plays, language barriers created some of the problem of transportation: New York audiences and critics had difficulty with the Cockney dialect Gems employed to convey Piaf's working-class origins, and London audiences had equal difficulty understanding the heavily colloquialised language of *for colored girls.* In both instances, rough edges that had engaged audiences in the 'home' countries were smoothed for 'foreign' audiences but this only succeeded in distancing those expecting less slick, more innovative work.

Misperceptions such as these of another culture's production values are not unique to feminist theatre. More troubling were the indications from reviews and conversations that the stories and contexts of *Piaf* and *for colored girls* did not carry across cultures. Despite their common concerns with autonomy, oppression, ambivalence towards men, and the need for community among women, and despite their very similar assertions of female sexuality, *Piaf*'s class consciousness puzzled American audiences whereas in *for colored girls* racial consciousness distanced English audiences. Gems and Shange, as well as Michelene Wandor and a growing number of female writers are now able to create models of women in community, but the evidence from audiences suggests that those communities may not yet transcend other bonds and contexts. The struggle to find what is personal, political and theatrical for *all* women and men continues.

7
Success and its Limits: Mary O'Malley, Wendy Wasserstein, Nell Dunn, Beth Henley, Catherine Hayes, Marsha Norman

Success in the theatre is most often measured by box-office receipts. The relationship of feminist drama to commerce and public attention in many ways follows a predictable pattern. While some of the most innovative and challenging plays by feminists are produced in obscure venues and are heralded by a relatively small group of supporters, the dramas by women that have achieved commercial success in the West End or Broadway tend to take fewer theatrical risks and to be less threatening to middle-class audiences than those performed on the fringe of the theatre establishment. Whether this pattern will continue is not yet clear, although it is increasingly apparent that feminist *scripts* are more subversive than the productions in which they are rendered in the large, commercial theatres.

This pattern is, of course, not exclusive to feminist drama. More than twenty-five years ago, Samuel Beckett's *Waiting for Godot* played to an audience of two in a tiny theatre in Paris; recently, a bill of two Beckett one-act plays enjoyed an extended run on Broadway. The history of theatre is haunted by similar public resistance to the strange and new and tempts the claim that the best drama is always a prophecy, a projection of how we will see the world not how it is seen at the moment. In most such instances, public and commercial resistance has both aesthetic and social grounds: the style of Ibsen's *A Doll's House* as well as Nora's exodus from her family provoked hostility and repression.

None the less, success for feminist plays is more problematic than has been the case for other avant-garde theatre. One need look no further than the failure to pass a mild-mannered Equal Rights Amendment in the United States to gauge the threat to social organisation posed by feminism. In Britain, where some progressive legislation has been passed, deeply imbedded biases against women still control institutional action, as Michelene Wandor's *Care and Control* makes clear. In both countries, commercial theatre's response to feminism has been consistent with that of other media: the most blatantly sexist images have been removed or modified, 'women's issues' have been put forward with a flourish, and a few productions by and about women have been mounted as tokens of recognition. Optimists perceive these gestures as necessary first steps that will pave the way for more challenging work; others, who have seen previous political movements dissipated by inoffensive liberalisations, fear that the appearance of change will assuage immediate anxieties but will ultimately undermine more revolutionary efforts.

With a few exceptions – most notably Ntozake Shange's *for colored girls*, Pam Gems's *Piaf* and Caryl Churchill's *Cloud Nine* – the 'hit' shows by and about women have rested on relatively safe terrain. Mary O'Malley's *Once a Catholic*, Wendy Wasserstein's *Uncommon Women and Others*, Nell Dunn's *Steaming*, Beth Henley's *Crimes of the*

Heart, Catherine Hayes *Skirmishes*, Marsha Norman's *Getting Out* and *'night, Mother*, have brought public recognition to their authors and have given large audiences an important window on the worlds of women. All of these plays focus on female characters and explore prevalent themes in feminist drama: mother–daughter relationships, sisterhood, sexuality and female autonomy. A common and not trivial attribute of these plays is their ability to make audiences laugh; each of these playwrights has a skill with dialogue and an eye for the absurd in ordinary life that make somber topics palatable and engaging. The weakness common to these plays is inherent in their particular strengths: no matter how serious the topic, they are all comedies of manners, revelations of the surfaces of sexual identity and sexism; they are not challenges to the deeper social structures that allow those manners to endure.

The first token in Britain of this form of success was Mary O'Malley's *Once a Catholic*, which opened at the Royal Court Theatre in 1977, and then moved to the Wyndham Theatre in the West End where it played for more than three years. In addition to its long run, it received high critical praise and numerous awards (although, like Gems's *Piaf*, not in the United States where negative reviews closed the show in a week). Like so many women playwrights, O'Malley had for many years combined writing with being a parent. Fringe theatre productions of a number of her one-act plays led to a residency at the Royal Court which in turn gave her the support to complete *Once a Catholic*.

Half of the fourteen characters in *Once a Catholic* are named Mary – Mary Mooney, Mary McGinty, Mary Gallagher, and so on – and they are all teenage students at a Catholic school for girls. In fact, all of the girls in Mother Peter's fifth-form class are named Mary, to the consternation of Mother Peter who asserts early in the play that 'No woman on this earth was ever worthy of the holy name of Mary.'

Most unworthy, in the judgement of the nuns who run the school, is Mary Mooney, a 'plain and scruffy' working-class Irish girl who is the centre of the play's attention. Mary is the victim of her own innocence: the nuns disbelieve her *naïveté*, an adolescent boy exploits it, her peers abuse it. More than anything, Mary Mooney wishes to become a nun herself, but in a world where, by definition, no earthly woman is genuinely virtuous, every move Mary makes is interpreted as a sign of corruption. When she asks what the Bible means by sodomy, the nuns assume she is taunting them; her confession of an afternoon of necking with Derek is perceived as arrogance not remorse and confusion. Even her talent as a singer is turned against her: she wishes to use her vocal gift to sing to God, but the head nun sees this skill as a sign that Mary is 'more the type to go into show business'.

It is possible to imagine a feminist production of *Once a Catholic*, but that is not the primary strategy of the play. O'Malley's stage world is not only specifically that of Catholic girls but is primarily an unveiling of the oppression and hypocrisy of the Church. Many themes and devices found in feminist drama are apparent in *Once a Catholic*, but the play is informed by the particular consciousness of Catholic women as Catholics not of women as women. Within the particular world of Irish Catholic culture, the spirit of women's rebellion against the sexual doctrines of the Church is forceful and important. O'Malley vividly captures the ambience of claustrophobia, of guilt and of relentless indoctrination that is extreme for women raised in the Catholic Church but is more subtly present for most women. That her 'Marys' subvert and question the roles defined for them signifies a distinct form of empowerment that is theatrically bold, especially in the context of West End production.

To accomplish this, however, O'Malley sacrifices the potential complexity of other women in the cast of *Once a Catholic*. The nuns are not presented as women but as representatives of an oppressive institution. Their repressed or neutralised sexuality is not an issue but a given. In contrast to Adrienne Kennedy's *A Lesson in Dead Language* in which we witness a grotesque vision of the education of young women, *Once a Catholic* takes a similar setting and renders it comically and critically but without exploration of the deep sources of sexual oppression.

The isolation of Mary Mooney, dramaturgically and thematically, also separates the play from ostensibly similar feminist dramas. While the device of having many Marys suggests the inclination away from specified individual characters, the other girls are less types than stereotypes, and the narrative emphasis is on Mary Mooney. The girls' school context, especially one dominated by nuns, provides an excellent setting for an exploration of the limits and possibilities of a community of women, but despite the bonds among a number of the girls, their main desire is to escape this all-female world. The girls compete with each other academically and socially; not one of Mary's peers acknowledges the difficulties posed for her by her naïveté or her parents' poverty. All of the men in the play are too weak to present any real threat to the women, but their treatment of the women, especially Mary Mooney, as objects is almost incidental to the play's strategy. *Once a Catholic* points to elements common to gender oppression, class oppression and religious oppression but the links among these remain vague. The final gesture of placing a large plastic phallus on the cross may be appropriately blasphemous but can also be too readily dismissed as an adolescent prank. Because the agents of this act are rebellious adolescents, the conjoining of phallus and cross is unlikely to assault the power of either icon and may unintentionally renew the potency of both.

Once a Catholic is not a failure nor is it a corruption of feminist theatre, it is just not enough. The positive aspect of its commercial success is that it makes us want more of O'Malley. Her next play *Look Out, Here Comes Trouble* explores the landscape of a mental institution and does probe more deeply into the dilemmas of women, especially in relation to men. Indicatively, this play never achieved the popular success of *Once a Catholic*.

What we learn from *Once a Catholic* is a confirmation for those inside and outside the experience of Catholic womanhood that adolescent Catholic girls are often reared in an atmosphere of sexual repression and hypocrisy and that most survive such educations by creating their own deceptions and manipulations. Although the class background and setting are very different, a similar, familiar lesson informs Wendy Wasserstein's *Uncommon Women and Others*, first produced in New York in 1977, the same year as the initial production of *Once a Catholic*. Much as O'Malley wrote her play from her own experience of a Catholic girls' school, Wasserstein's drama is drawn from her experiences at Mt Holyoke College, a prestigious private institution for women.

With the minimal exception of the ironic frame provided by a male voice-over, *Uncommon Women* also shares with *Once a Catholic* a conventionally realistic style, ornamented by comic hyperbole. Much like Tennessee Williams's *The Glass Menagerie*, *Uncommon Women* uses memory as a structural device: the play begins and ends with the reunion of five women who had been classmates six years earlier at college; most of the drama is set in a dormitory living-room during the women's student days. In addition to the five women at the reunion, the college housemother and three other women students join the cast in the dormitory scenes.

Uncommon Women has even less plot than does *Once a Catholic*, and like O'Malley's drama the play relies on clever dialogue to convey the ambience of a particular world of women. The talk is witty and, much like an early seventies consciousness-raising group, focuses on complaints and confusions particular to women struggling for self-awareness. The women are only 'uncommon', however, in their privileged position in the upper-middle and upper classes of American society. Within that world, they and their talk are recognisably embarrassing stereotypes of female college students: Samantha is a 'child–woman' who will use her little talents to give support to a husband; Rita is the wild adventuress who treats sex like a commodity; Carter is a silent intellectual who wants to make a film of Wittgenstein's philosophy. Six years after their graduation, each of these women is in an utterly predictable situation. *Uncommon Women* confirms the last message from the unseen male voice: 'Society has trained women from childhood to accept a limited set of options and restricted levels of aspirations.'[1] The play offers no alternatives to or substantial critique *of* that message. To the contrary, the women are so amusing and banal that other options seem irrelevant.

Nell Dunn's *Steaming*, a West End hit in 1981–2 that also suffered a brief run in New York, continues the pattern of gathering an all-female cast of characters in a setting that, by definition, excludes men. This time, the location is a women's public bath, occupied by Violet, the matron, and five women patrons. The City Council's threatened closing of the baths provides a simple plot structure; in this play, also, it is the ambience of this 'women's space' and the stories the women tell each other that fill the theatrical space.

Unlike *Once a Catholic* and *Uncommon Women*, *Steaming* engages us in the individual lives of its characters and suggests the possibility of community among them. Class and gender are presented as intertwined and parallel sources of oppression and are given solid dramatic form in the large and small transformations of each of the women. Josie, the play's most compelling character, is caught at the beginning of the play between her disgust with the menial, fatiguing jobs available to her as an uneducated woman and her anger at the alternative – economic dependence on men who exploit her sexually.

Dawn, a strangely childlike woman in her mid-thirties, also suggests the terror of a trapped animal at the beginning of the play, but her anger is wholly and pathologically repressed. We gradually learn that at some point in the past, Dawn was raped by an officer in the police station where she worked; since that time, she has been in and out of mental hospitals and under the infantalising care of her equally repressed sixty-five-year-old mother.

The challenge of saving the bathhouse, of preserving this rare refuge for working-class women, empowers all of the women but serves as a special inspiration for Josie and Dawn. The women lose their appeal to refurbish rather than destroy the baths, but in daring to plead their case in public, both Josie and Dawn realise a competence neither had previously achieved. The final image of these women taking turns swinging on a Tarzan-rope over and into the bath captures both the new-found strength of each individual and the power they have found in mutual support.

One of the strengths of *Steaming* is its almost aggressive

focus on mature women. The plays risks disturbing audience biases by requiring us to acknowledge the naked
bodies of women over thirty-five. Unfortunately, in the
West End production, rather than establishing the common
vulnerability of women, nudity was used to titillate the
audience. The act of disrobing was played to the audience
with an inappropriate coyness; lighting, blocking and
costuming called attention to breasts; and pacing called
attention to the rarity of undressing on stage. *Steaming*
yields, unnecessarily, to one of the dangers of feminist
theatre, that it makes the audience voyeurs of secret
women's worlds rather than participant–observers in a
complex social–sexual structure. With *Once a Catholic* and
Uncommon Women spectators are necessarily and unre-
flectively voyeurs. Because a public bath, like a girls'
school, does by its nature exclude men, it, too, is vulnerable
to a voyeurism that demeans those on-stage as well as the
audience. This need not be the case, however, because
Dunn's characters bring enough of the outside world with
them to remind us of a broader landscape. But by playing
for laughs, especially in the exaggeration of Dawn's mental
illness, and delivering speeches as set pieces of 'feminism',
the production forced a condescending distance on the
audience that made the personal trivial and apolitical.

A similar trivialisation was accomplished with a New
York hit of the early eighties, Beth Henley's *Crimes of the
Heart*. Winner of the Pulitzer Prize for Drama, *Crimes of
the Heart* was first produced by the Actors' Theater of
Louisville, a residential theatre company that in recent
years has become a leading supporter of new plays,
especially those by women. By the time it moved to
Broadway in 1981, *Crimes of the Heart* was already a
success from numerous productions across the country and
off-Broadway.

The script of *Crimes of the Heart* has many of the ingredients of a strong feminist drama. Three sisters gather in the kitchen of a small house in rural Mississippi. They have come together for the first time in many years on what happens to be the thirtieth birthday of Lenny, the oldest sister, because the youngest of them, Babe, has shot her husband in the stomach. We eventually discover that prior to the shooting, Babe's husband had found her talking with a fifteen-year-old black boy with whom Babe had, in fact, been making love. For Babe, however, shooting Zachary, her husband, has little to do with her affair: as she tells it to her sisters, she just did not like Zachary's looks. Babe thus shares with other female characters in feminist drama the experience of a moment when she looks at a man whose bed she has shared or is about to share and feels utter revulsion. Often, as is clear in Fornes's *Fefu and Her Friends* and Gems's *Dusa, Fish, Stas and Vi*, the intensity of that revulsion is such that the woman is torn between self-destruction and violence towards the man. Babe's first instinct, we learn, was to shoot herself but, recalling how her own mother had hung herself, she recognises that she wants to live but wants Zachary dead.

Where Fornes's and Gems's plays demand that women seek new ways of relating to each other and to men, the unravelling of *Crimes of the Heart* encourages the audience to be hostile towards men but leaves little alternative – for men or women – other than to shoot any male who displays chauvinistic tendencies. There is a potential in Henley's play, similar to that in these other works, for sisterhood as a constructive resource, but that is undermined, particularly in the Broadway production, by the behaviour of the sisters themselves. Lonely, generous Lenny's only moment of triumph comes when she gets the courage to call a male friend and confess that she cut off their relationship because she was afraid to admit her inability to have children. More is made of her difficulty in making the call than in her internalisation of the stigma of one 'bad' ovary, and only at the very end of the play does one of her sisters try to refute Lenny's image of herself as an old maid. Meg, the middle sister, confirms the town's belief that she is a 'loose' woman by spending her first night home with an old beau, now married to another woman, but when she 'confesses' this as well as the truth about her non-existent Hollywood singing career, her sisters' response is hysterical laughter. Babe and Lenny can only see the irony of Meg's timing because they have just come from the hospital where Grandaddy, to whom Meg wants to admit the truth, has just lapsed into a coma. Even Babe's authentically courageous attempt to shelter the identity of her young lover is unappreciated by her sisters.

Because the play's texture relies on the characterisations of the three sisters and the dialogue among them, it can only move the audience if the ordinariness of the women is made specific and honest in performance. In the Broadway production, however, each of the actresses parodied her role, exaggerating the 'Southernness' of the women, the *naïveté* of Lenny, the brashness of Babe and the pseudo-urban sophistication of Meg. Laughing at these women is boring and allows a particularly dangerous condescension when the audience's frame is a play by and about women. Once this ambience is established, Babe's desire to play the saxophone, even if she learns the skill in jail, becomes ludicrous where it might have been a potent sign of a woman's wish for competence. A production that plays too obviously for laughs belittles Meg's vision at the end of the play of one brief moment in which the sisters are together, laughing. The vision is not an inspiration but a redundancy. Women and men may need to laugh at the absurdity of their roles, and feminists may need some relief from their vigil, but it is difficult to share in the laughter of women who have yielded to caricatures and made themselves objects of derision.

Sisters reunited in a time of family crisis are also the subject of a London hit of the eighties, Catherine Hayes's *Skirmishes*. High praise from critics and good box-office brought it from the Liverpool Playhouse Upstairs to a long run at the Hampstead Theatre in London and then to the Manhattan Theater Club where it continued to receive laudatory reviews. Comparing it favourably to Dunn's *Steaming* and Churchill's *Top Girls*, New York critics seemed relieved by Hayes's compassion for her characters and witty but unambiguous dialogue.

Skirmishes is more immediately accessible to spectators than many feminist dramas, in part because its context, the impending death of the mother of two daughters, is an almost irresistible frame for empathy and tension. *Skirmishes* takes a familiar, realistic approach to its subject, and, as in *Crimes of the Heart*, humorous and ironic dialogue relieves the sobriety of the situation but also risks over-indulgence at the expense of the characters. Hayes's sisters are 'types' of women: Jean, the sister who has stayed at home caring for her invalid mother, has much in common with Henley's Lenny, and Rita, the sister who has previously managed to avoid visits home, takes her own share of the narcissism given to Meg in *Crimes of the Heart*. None of the sisters in these plays communicate well with each other, although in *Skirmishes* this is confronted as a central issue, more in the manner of Churchill's *Top Girls* than Henley's *Crimes of the Heart*.

The tensions between Jean and Rita in *Skirmishes* were symbolised in production by placing one sister to the right and one sister to the left of the mother's bed which sat centre-stage. Mother, particularly in her dying, separates her daughters, while at the same time emblemising their structural connection. We, like Jean and Rita, must stare at Mother and death for the uninterrupted hour and a half of the play. For Jean and Rita, this unyielding presence is a medium for expression of differences in values, histories and feelings about death itself. Jean's isolation and total responsibility for her mother have made her bitter, self-pitying and eager for her mother's death. Rita's obsession with her own children and her unease with illness serve her well as excuses for her absence. Jean's clinical descriptions and practical talk about funerals and property repulse Rita who neither has nor wants the callousness her sister has acquired.

The appeal of *Skirmishes* lies in the candour with which the sisters address each other and their ability, almost despite themselves, to strip their veneers and admit to their parallel frustration with their lives. There is an honesty, too, in the play's movement towards a recognition scene that is never complete; after looking and talking past each other for most of the play, each sister admits the failure of her marital relationship. Jean concludes this exchange with the declaration that 'Once you've lost their eyes, it's no use.' The two sisters then look at each other, but just as they begin this mutual acknowledgement Mother awakens, commanding, 'Rita, you take everything.' At the end, with Mother's death, Jean leaves the room. For these two sisters, there is neither the reversal that traditionally accompanies recognition scenes nor the transformation that affirms new possibilities. The mother's dying moments are harsh and unheroic, and her death will release her daughters only from their immediate burdens but not from the deeper futility of their lives.

While *Skirmishes* takes a relentlessly photographic

approach to a private, intimate scene, it complicates our voyeuristic perspective through the continuous presence of the mother. It is never clear, to Rita as well as to the audience, just how much Mother is seeing, hearing or sensing and, because of that ambiguity, she serves as a silent witness to the interaction between Jean and Rita. Because Mother oversees the action on stage, like a leader of an unseen chorus, she provides an almost public perspective that makes the audience responsible in and to the world as it is portrayed.

Within the context of feminist drama the omissions of *Skirmishes* are vivid and disappointing. There is no completed moment of affection between the sisters nor is there explanation of this absence. Ambivalences towards children and nurturing roles are honestly displayed, but the accumulation of negative images of mothers leaves little space for reconstructive notions of mothering. Perhaps most frustrating is the play's unfulfilled potential for a powerful polyphony. Because of the stable, balanced structure of *Skirmishes*, it initially suggests an equality and diversity of female voices, including the almost-mute 'voice' of the mother. Instead of this polyphony, Jean commands the household, controls the dialogue, and thus controls the play's point of view in much the way that Lillian Hellman's female characters limit access to the worlds they inhabit. We know little of Rita that Jean does not elicit, and Mother becomes a passive receptacle for us as she has been for Jean. The play is thus successful in establishing one woman's world and world-view but hesitates to take the leap from a play about a woman to a drama that reconstitutes theatrical and political strategies.

A remarkably similar claustrophobic stage space and dramaturgy define the biggest recent hit by an American woman playwright, Marsha Norman's *'night, Mother.*

Throughout the performance of *'night, Mother*, a mother and her adult daughter manoeuvre around each other and around the daughter's opening announcement that she is planning on killing herself that evening. The static setting for this encounter is a stereotyped American kitchen-family room that never escapes the ambience of afternoon television soap-opera.

Two years after Beth Henley's success with *Crimes of the Heart*, *'night, Mother* brought Marsha Norman the distinction of becoming the second woman in twenty-five years to receive the Pulitzer Prize in Drama. The play was first performed in Boston at the American Repertory Theater before moving to Broadway in the spring of 1983. The awarding of the Pulitzer Prize, coupled with praise and numerous productions of her first play *Getting Out*, placed Norman in the public eye to a degree that has been rare for women playwrights. She appeared on the cover of the *New York Times Magazine* on 1 May 1983, received the prestigious Susan Smith Blackburn Prize, a new award explicitly for English-speaking women playwrights, and quickly became a symbol of what the *New York Times* called 'the new voices in the theater.'

Norman's voice, like Henley's, was first heard in Louisville, her hometown as well as the home of the Actors' Theater. She developed the script of *Getting Out* from her memory of a woman she had met while she was working with mentally disturbed people at a state hospital. The most powerful invention of this script is its dramatic embodiment of a particularly female form of schizophrenia. Taking a polyphonous approach, Norman created two central characters: Arlene, the 'good', constructive persona of a woman sent to prison for second-degree murder, robbery, forgery and prostitution, and Arlie, the 'bad' destructive persona of the same woman. Performed by two different actresses, Arlene is, in ordinary critical terms, the protagonist and Arlie the antagonist of the drama. Norman's strategy leads us to rethink these terms and the assumptions behind them. By definition, a protagonist is singular; he or she is the 'first' actor. This has come to mean the main character of a drama and the instigator of action in a play. In *Getting Out*, however, Arlie and Arlene are each initiators, each is dependent on the other, and neither is genuinely 'first'.

The mythos of female identity symbolised by this divided persona extends the play's world well beyond the prison and dingy apartment in which *Getting Out* is set. Throughout the performance, two periods and locations of Arlie–Arlene's life play concurrently. Centre-stage is the one-room apartment to which Arlene has come after her release from prison. Almost completely surrounding the apartment, on raised levels, are the prison catwalk, Arlie's cell and other prison spaces. Past and present, captivity and liberty, 'bad' woman and 'good' thus occupy the same theatrical time and adjacent space. Arlene is the reformed, controlled persona whose good behaviour as defined by prison mores has led to the character's release; more than anything, Arlene wants to see the child she bore but never knew. Arlie was always in trouble, unable to express the confusion and pain of repeated abuse except in verbal and physical violence towards herself and others. Arlie has transformed into Arlene, but in this unique interpolation of transformations, the original role does not vanish with change. Arlene cannot simply walk away from Arlie but must accept her and the knowledge she possesses. In *Getting Out*, transformation is not a magical but historical process, suggestive of new directions for dramatic realism.

Much of what Arlie knows but represses is her history of sexual exploitation by men: her father seduced her when she was a child and, since that time, a series of men including the prison guard who brings her 'home' have used and confused her. Arlie was complicit in these relationships primarily because she could not imagine herself as an independent person. The key to the successful resolution of the conflicts between Arlie and Arlene is the friendship offered by Ruby, herself an ex-convict who lives upstairs from Arlene's apartment. Ruby knows all the lines men use and protects Arlene–Arlie from their seduction. Equally important, Ruby knows the terror of solitude and the frustration of menial jobs; she serves as a positive model of a woman with few skills or resources who can survive and offer support to another with recompense.

One of the unresolved symbolic prisons of Arlie–Arlene's life is her relationship with her mother who visits her shortly after Arlene's prison release. Mother, a cab driver, tries awkwardly to nurture her daughter with gifts of coloured towels and a bedspread and fervent attempts to sweep up the apartment. She negates these gestures, however, with repeated criticisms of Arlene's appearance and behaviour. Mother has come out of duty to the daughter she still sees as a 'hateful brat', and she can neither see nor give what Arlene needs – an embrace and support for her struggle to change.

Mother vanishes from the stage after her one brief visit, leaving anger and anguish in her daughter and an irritating sense of incompletion in the audience. As if in acknowledgement that this does not suffice, Norman returns to and isolates the mother–daughter relationship in *'night, Mother*. Reversing the power structure of *Getting Out*, Jessie, the daughter in *'night, Mother*, is the woman putting things in order and threatening what her mother sees as desertion. The housekeeping is as much a duty for Jessie as it was for Arlene's mother, but the threat here is more final

and deliberate. Where Arlene decided for life, as unre-
warding as it might be for a woman of her history and class,
Jessie has decided to kill herself. She is convinced that
suicide is the only authentic act available to her. Her death
will ensure freedom from the imprisonment of suffocating
monotony and her mother's liberation from dependency
and responsibility. Jessie spends the hours before her
suicide fulfilling what she believes is her responsibility to
her mother; she explains her resolve, instructs her mother
in the maintenance of the house, and rebuffs her mother's
attempts to dissuade her.

Perhaps the soap-opera dialogue and setting of *'night,
Mother* are intended to make us understand that the daily
lives of ordinary women are far less glamorous and far
more unhappy than is revealed in the television drama that
serves as the main contemporary source of dramatic images
of women. Yet at least in the New York production, the
absence of genuine contact between mother and daughter
served intellectually to support the necessity of Jessie's
suicide while impairing my ability to grieve or feel anger.
Mother's deployment of all her wit and will against her
daughter's suicide is a kind of liberation, but it also
ironically separates her from sorrow and affection.

Norman implied in a *New York Times Magazine*
interview that Jessie's 'gift of knowledge' to her mother
demonstrated 'the most profound kind of love'. But for
Jessie who cannot find one thing she likes enough to make
living worthwhile neither knowledge nor love suffice. Why,
then, should we believe they do for others? If one message
of this play is that many women perceive no contexts for
action or control, then the sheltered space of the family-
room must be extended to reveal the real constraints
outside. The more troubling message, not of the play itself
but of its success, is that the most appealing role for the

audience continues to be that of the voyeur. 'It's a time of great exploration of secret worlds, of worlds that have been kept quiet', Norman said at the end of the *New York Times* interview.[2] On stage, such worlds allow us not just to know secrets but to remain secreted ourselves. As *'night, Mother* ironically makes clear, knowledge is not sufficient, and off-stage suicide does not transform society. It denies it.

8
Nooks, Crannies and New Directions: Collective Scripts, Gay Drama, Feminist Dramas by Men and the Example of Wendy Kesselman

At a time in history when most people in the Western world experience drama through television sets, when the majority of commercial productions are revivals, and when no play since *Waiting for Godot* has become a part of our cultural vocabulary, claims about the emergence of a new form of drama for live theatre should be suspect. Whether or not it is useful to label the plays discussed in this book under the category 'feminist drama', I continue to be surprised by the sheer quantity and diversity of scripts that explore our needs and our limitations in thinking of ourselves as women and men. Feminist drama is unquestionably one of the most tenacious and resonant forms of discourse about sexual politics. Theatre is a fertile home for feminists, at least for the moment, because so many of the issues of feminism – role-playing, relationships to others, individuality and collectivity, power, authority, responsibility, production and reproduction – are also the issues of theatre.

Any attempt, then, to 'conclude' my discussion of

feminist drama would be inappropriate. Instead, these last pages are devoted to surveying some 'nooks and crannies', some other hills in the landscape that should at least appear on the map. Plays by collectives or ensemble theatre companies designate one such area that merits attention as a substantial source of energy. Many spectators identify feminist theatre with a production or productions created from text to performance by a company. Few of the scripts from these productions are publicly available, and they serve more as records of an event than scores for re-production. The performance energy of many collaborative productions is a key to their success, perhaps because the participation of the performers in the research, storytelling and improvisations ensures a sense of responsibility for whatever is presented to the audience. Often scripts written by a collective are verbally inelegant, strategically vague and inseparable from a particular cause or moment in history. None the less, productions generated by collective scripting are often more exciting and more engaging for audiences than those based on beautiful texts. As a director who has worked with collective scripting as well as with productions of the classics of English-language theatre, I have noticed that performers who create their own scripts know what they are doing on stage at every moment, whereas even the best actor often speaks a line from a 'masterpiece' without a full grasp of what the words mean.

Capturing in print that clarity and energy achieved in theatre ensemble work is difficult, partly because those who created the script assume understandings that evolved in rehearsal. Narrative introductions to published 'company' scripts can be helpful in this regard. The introduction to the published text of Red Ladder Theatre's *Strike While the Iron is Hot* notes that the play was their first attempt at a 'Women's Play' and that it evolved in a climate of changing consciousness among the men and women in the company as well as the audience. Members of the company were divided in their understandings of the root problems surrounding the play's topic, women and work. For some, patriarchy was the major obstacle to the liberation of women, while for others class conflict was primary. The final script assaults both male domination of women and the exploitation of women as members of the working class. It attempts to sustain the dialectical process by juxtaposing these points of view. Two banners are flown at the end of the production. One reads 'Women will never be free while workers are in chains.' The other reads 'Workers will never be free while women are in chains.' Episodes and songs illustrate both points of view with no attempt to resolve the conflict or persuade the audience towards either argument. In developing the script, the Red Ladder Company discussed these contrasting perspectives at length; the result was both a moderation of extreme positions and an encapsulation of the process: in performance, the actors were continuing their dialogue. This poses a challenge and a constraint for re-production: *Strike While the Iron is Hot* could appear disjointed and confusing in performance, a flat presentation of alternatives, unless each acting company reinitiates the discussion. But as each production company rethinks the issues, new balances will be struck and the script altered for each subsequent production.

Because collectively created scripts are from the start generated by dialogue and committed to polyphony, there is often a more fluid notion of a script and less pressure towards a 'final' version. In a number of instances, including Red Ladder's production of *Strike While the Iron is Hot*, this has led to substantial script changes in response to audience reaction. As the audience for *Strike While the Iron is Hot* broadened and was no longer primarily trade union and women's groups, the company added a number of new songs to make more of a 'show' and 'enrich the rhythms of the audience's involvement'.[1]

A striking instance of audience-motivated script alteration occurred in the early seventies with *The Independent Female*, the first 'feminist' production of the San Francisco Mime Troupe. Highly respected for its rigour and ingenuity, the Mime Troupe has been committed to political theatre for the last twenty-five years. While major credit for the script of *The Independent Female* is given to *one* of the company members, Joan Holden, accounts of the production emphasise that this was one of the first collective creations of the Mime Troupe. As was the case with Red Ladder, when the Mime Troupe decided in 1970 to turn their attention to feminist issues, there was no clear political line even among the newly conscious women in the troupe. After internal discussion and consultation with members of the San Francisco Bay Area's women's movement, the company arrived at a satirical melodrama that depicts the transformation of 'beautiful, innocent but impressionable Gloria' from slave to 'independent female'.

In its first incarnation, *The Independent Female* presented Gloria's conflict through the opposition of her grossly chauvinistic fiance, John, and a rabidly feminist 'career-woman', Sarah. The original version of the play ended with Gloria's surrender to her husband and to his image of the perfect wife as 'the most precious thing a man owns'. That version intended to make the audience laugh at the extremes of sexism and feminism while making the 'natural' melodramatic ending so obviously wrong that it would be unacceptable to the audience. The play's strategy was not sufficiently clear to actors or spectators; stereotypes were still too rampant to be easy sources of laughter. Feminists who saw early performances objected to the caricatured depiction of the feminist, Sarah, and to the defeatism implied in Gloria's capitulation. If the company believed that Sarah represented a paranoid fantasy rather than a genuine feminist, this was not apparent in performance. Nor was the company's critical attitude towards the play's conclusion coherent. In response, Holden and the Mime Troupe rewrote the script. Sarah became more appealing, and the ending was reversed such that Gloria celebrates her liberation and promises to fight for others. In the second version, Gloria's self-victimised mother exits with her daughter, with fist raised for battle. With those changes, the play became a hit, not only for the Mime Troupe but in productions throughout the country by dozens of theatre companies.

A similar flexibility in response to audience commentary has been apparent in The Women's Theatre Group, one of the oldest London feminist companies. Its 1974 production of *My Mother Says I Never Should* actually utilised ideas from the intended audience of teenagers *before* the script was performed. For a production on the 'double standards', members of the company talked with girls, teachers and parents, 'then we pooled our information, created characters and a plot, improvised, and finally went in twos and threes to write and rewrite'.[2] The play that resulted, deliberately written in the style of television situation comedy, depicts the familiar but usually hidden encounters of adolescent females with their own sexuality. One of the two teenage girls in the play, Wendy, misses her period, and, after discovering that she is not pregnant, decides to take contraceptive pills. The play is unashamedly didactic, aimed at informing adolescent audiences of their options of their ability to choose. The closing verse indicates both the tone and the message of the production:

> We've been talking to you about choices
> 'Cause some day we think you'll find:
> If you don't control your body
> Somebody's gonna screw your mind.[3]

My Mother Says I Never Should shares with other collectively written pieces an emphasis on ritual both as form and subject. At the Spring 1983 Women's Theater Festival in Santa Cruz, California, more than half the productions addressed female rituals and many attempted a ritualistic ambience that would call forth the participation of the audience. Recurrent rites ranging from daily activities such as washing and ironing to critical events such as the onset of menstruation or giving birth, provide accessible frames for inexperienced writers while calling attention to important but often trivialised aspects of every woman's life. The Women's Theatre Group's *Time Pieces* overtly articulates this inclination by constructing the play around a girl's sixteenth birthday party to which her aunt brings a family photograph album. The ensemble presents dramatised anecdotes evoked by the photographs of the girl's female ancestors, giving her and the audience the gift of history, especially as it is filled with positive models of women.

At the Foot of the Mountain, one of the strongest American collective feminist theatre companies, also emphasises ritual in its productions. Many of their shows, whose 'scores' are usually put in final form by Martha Boesing, deliberately combine scripted drama with invocations to the audience. Whereas various attempts in the sixties to address the audience directly often confused and distressed spectators, these invitations to the audience are more successful because they are located in women's history and are presented as an attempt to renew ancient ritualistic devices, such as chants and dance, important to women.

Transformation as confirmation of ritual and extension of feminist dramaturgical principles is especially vivid in At the Foot of the Mountain's *The Story of a Mother, A Ritual Drama*. Described by Boesing as 'a kaleidoscope of images which expores the relationship between mothers and daughters',[4] the event begins with the appearance of The Big Mother, a figure created by one actress sitting on another's shoulders; the two are covered by a long dress and apron. Even the scenes intended to be performed solely by the actresses are published only as outlines and suggestions for improvisation. The script provides other groups with a set of concepts, arranged strategically to reverse natural life-order. By beginning with the loss of the Mother in a section called 'Mourning' and ending with 'Birthing' and a ritual called 'communion', in which performers offer bread to the audience, the production acknowledges death and separation of mothers and daughters but leaves the audience with an affirmation of re-creation and continuity.[5]

In the late seventies, a number of feminist companies committed to collective scripting focused their plays on the struggles of lesbian women. These groups, as well as individual playwrights, have raised the issue of the relation of gay drama to feminist drama. The instances in which feminist drama includes homosexual and heterosexual relationships within one frame – Churchill's *Cloud Nine* and Fornes's *Fefu and Her Friends* are two examples – are sufficiently potent to suggest that gay and feminist politics do not necessitate divergent categories of drama.

A comparison of two plays by American playwright Susan Miller does reveal, however, a subtle but distinct difference between what might be called a 'straight' feminist drama and a 'gay' feminist drama. Both plays use the metaphor of a journey to give a structure to the changes in the lives and self-awareness of the central female characters. Perry, the protagonist of *Cross Country*, is a teacher, writer and mother who leaves her husband, child and university job in the mid-west to travel to California and establish her own autonomy. In the middle of her journey, she has two lesbian affairs, one with a neighbour whom she deeply loves, the other with a student whose affection is more sensual and superficial. Near the end of the play, Perry is alone, about to attend a rehearsal of her first play. Perry's sexual relationships with women are important to her journey but no more so than her solitude or her relationship with her husband. *Cross-Country* experiments with an inventive form of collaboration in presenting the script as a series of episodes and pieces of dialogue that need to be finished by the production company. Each group of performers can therefore choose whether or not to emphasise the lesbian relationships, allowing for *Cross-Country* to be presented as either 'straight' or 'gay' feminist drama.

While Miller's *Confessions of a Female Disorder* tells a similar story of a woman's developing autonomy and self-awareness, it moves irrevocably towards a 'confession' of love between two women. The final, silent scene of the play excludes the men in the cast while the women 'take over the room' in 'an exploration, an unearthing, a transference' that is an erotic expression of their control of the space and their attraction to each other. This last scene is in part an affirmation of the connection between autonomy and community. But whereas spectators and even actresses have missed the sexual attraction between the women characters in *Cross-Country*, no one is allowed

174

to mistake the women's relationships in *Confessions of a Female Disorder* for non-erotic friendship.

On the other hand, there are plays that are intended primarily for male and female homosexual audiences. Gay Sweatshop's 1978 productions in Britain of *What the Hell is She Doing Here?* and *Iceberg*, both collectively written (although only the women worked on the first), were intended for consciousness-raising among the lesbian and male homosexual communities. American playwright Jane Chambers has written a number of feminist plays on sexual violence and the treatment of women as objects, but her best-known work, *A Late Snow*, is devoted to the exploration of love-affairs among women. By presenting lesbian characters without suggesting the need to justify their sexual choices, *A Late Snow* explicitly offers lesbian women a rare opportunity to acknowledge and examine their relationships as personal as well as social problems.

In his introduction to the anthology *Gay Plays*, William M. Hoffman makes a useful distinction between 'gay drama', which he defines as plays *about* homosexuality, and 'gay theatre', which he defines as a manner of production, applicable to any drama, in which actors and audience mutually and overtly acknowledge their homosexuality.[6] Plays like *What the Hell is She Doing Here?* and *A Late Snow* can by this definition be performed as 'gay drama', without requiring performers to make sexually explicit gestures to spectators as they would in gay theatre. Alternatively, some performances of Churchill's *Cloud Nine* became gay theatre when male actors made no attempt to play female roles convincingly but rather reminded the audience that they were men dressed up as women and used this reminder to flirt with other men in the audience.

Gay drama by men rarely coincides with feminist drama. A remarkable exception to this tendency is American playwright Len Berkman's *'Til the Beatles Reunite*, a conventionally realistic drama about an unconventional household comprised of two men, one a widower and one a *divorcé*, and their teenage daughters. Shortly after the death of David's wife, Brian's wife leaves him and the two men move in together. David and Brian grow more intimate, and combative, and finally discuss Brian's unrequited sexual attraction to David.

Besides the complex role-playing of David and Brian, Berkman's play is concerned with the struggles of growing up female as presented in the two daughters, Ruth and Piper. By placing these girls in a context of a household without mothers, Berkman avoids the clichés of female adolescence and gently unveils the strengths and the vulnerabilities of young women. From their naïve perspective, Ruth and Piper are able to perceive the erotic element in the love between their fathers as readily as they perceive it between men and women. While it is a lesson learned and taught with pain, Ruth and Piper also teach their fathers that to admit to a need for a mother, for a woman to guide and nurture them, is not to negate the love they have for their fathers. In keeping with many feminist dramas, *'Til the Beatles Reunite* is a morality play about right and wrong, showing admirable and despicable behaviour between men and men, women and women and men and women. One of the few male playwrights who identifies himself as a feminist, Berkman displays in his drama opposition to rigid distinctions between gender roles.

American male playwrights such as Michael Weller and Tom Eyen, who have been hailed for the attention their plays pay to women, may sometimes point in the direction of feminist drama but the women in their plays are at best victims of oppressive social institutions and media hype and at worst objects of their own self-loathing. By contrast, Berkman addresses many of the structural issues raised by contemporary women playwrights, sometimes contributing an angle of vision less available to women. *Voila: Rape in Technicolor* views the landscape of contemporary America as inhabited by a rape culture. The terror of violence and assault expressed in Shange's *Three Pieces* here becomes a constant of middle-class life, evident in the rage of a woman who has been literally raped, in the assaultive behaviour of a student, and in advertisement images that barely disguise the exploitation of male and female bodies.

Perhaps because of the influence of feminism on socialist theatre, there are more instances in Britain of feminist drama by men. In particular, the work of Steve Gooch, Stephen Lowe and David Rudkin merits attention. Since the early seventies, Gooch has been writing plays about women's individual and collective strength, often placing the struggles of his characters in historical contexts that parallel contemporary situations. *Female Transport*, his first overtly feminist drama, takes place on a nineteenth-century ship carrying convicts to Australia. During the awful journey, the six women who share a tiny cell learn how to improvise from minimal resources, and also learn that the community they have established among themselves can continue even when they no longer share the same space. Gooch's *The Women Pirates: Ann Bonney and Mary Read* arrives at a similarly positive conclusion in its reconstruction of the history of two women pirates who create an 'alternative' community outside the sexist and imperialistic laws of conventional society.

Stephen Lowe's work is more lyrical and less assertively political than Gooch's or Berkman's; nor has Lowe written a body of work that could be called feminist. There are few plays, however, by women or men that articulate and evoke such profound respect for women as does Lowe's 1978 *Touched*. Framed in time by VE day and VJ day at the end of the Second World War, *Touched* turns our attention to the unheralded victories and defeats of working-class women who wait out the war in an industrial city. Lowe avoids sentimentality through Brechtian conventions: ticker-tapes across the proscenium arch and radio announcements persistently remind the audience that his characters live not only on the stage and in our knowledge of them but in history. The 'curtain' of bedsheets drying on a clothesline opens on the almost bare stage and barer lives of a family of women who have been physically and emotionally undernourished while the men fight the enemy abroad. One of the women, whose husband is due to arrive home shortly, announces to her sister that she is pregnant, and this pregnancy becomes the informing metaphor of the play. With few men not in the army, the only possible fathers of this child are a mentally retarded young man who happily claims paternity or a German prisoner-of-war confined nearby. The pregnancy is a fantasy, an embodi- ment of the woman's desire for creation in the face of a world destroyed, for life in the face of the media's unrelenting reports of death. Her conception is so fully willed that it takes on its own vitality. One of the most powerful scenes in contemporary drama occurs when the pregnant woman is gently undressed by her sister and led naked to a hot bath intended to bring on a miscarriage. Unlike dozens of exploitative theatrical nude scenes, and in contrast to the female nudity in Dunn's *Steaming*, this image of a naked woman perfectly articulates the dignity and vulnerability of the female self.

Pregnancy is also the central metaphor for another

powerful feminist drama by a male playwright, David Rudkin's *Ashes*. Anne and Colin, the central characters, try desperately to conceive a child and are only able to do so by allowing themselves to become experimental objects of modern technology. Before the end of the play, however, Anne miscarries. Both *Touched* and *Ashes* confront the most elemental human desires for self-respect, for meaning, for re-production, and for society with others. Rudkin makes the personal infertility of Anne and Colin a dynamic image of the political impotence of individuals in the power struggles of Northern Ireland. Thematically, the specifically personal becomes political through the transformation of Colin from a man who accepts his culture's criteria for manhood to a man who can accept nurturance and vulnerability and reject aggression and violence. The richness of Rudkin's drama lies in the startling and resonant imagery of its language; on stage the speeches of the play resound like song and are in perfect harmony with the persistent injections of modern music that occur throughout the performance. While neither *Touched* nor *Ashes* employs the overt transformational conventions that so often identify feminist dramas, the miraculous pregnancy of *Touched* and the 'shedding' of the 'male personae' that concludes *Ashes* encourage the possibility of authentic change not just in the theatre but in the world.

These vital signs of feminist visions in plays written by men raise the possibility that feminist drama may yet become the model for most theatre and not just one genre among many. It would be foolish, none the less, to overestimate the significance of these few feminist plays by men, and perhaps even more unwise to overlook the clear evidence that playwrights like Berkman, Gooch, Lowe and Rudkin, writing from what remains the dominant gender perspective, are far more positive than most of their women colleagues about the possibilities for change in either theatre or society.

Neither constructive models nor beautiful scenes are enough. That, at least, is the challenge of the most recent feminist playwrights, and it is nowhere more apparent than in the first play of a young American woman named Wendy Kesselman. Kesselman's *My Sister in this House* is a powerful drama and a vivid symbol of theatre's ability to demonstrate changes in points of view. The play is based on a historical incident that occurred in Le Mans, France, in 1933, an event that previously inspired Jean Genet's *The Maids*. Not coincidentally, it was to Genet that Kate Millett turned for a constructive example in the first chapter of her book *Sexual Politics*, a book that in 1970 was synonymous with the women's movement. A comparison of Genet's play with Kesselman's makes clear how quickly and deeply our resources for theatrical models of sexual politics have been enriched by feminist drama.

Two sisters, Lea and Christine Papin, both of whom had been employed as maids in the same household for years, suddenly turn and kill their mistress and her daughter. Genet took this event and twisted it back on the sisters, removing from them the responsibility for murder while at the same time making them grotesque victims of their own self-loathing. In *The Maids*, the sisters, renamed Claire and Solange, play a game in which they murder their mistress, but when their various 'pretend' games are over, Claire poisons herself as a gift to her sister who takes credit for murder and goes gleefully to the guillotine. The Mistress has no daughter in Genet's play, but she does have a male lover who controls the world of the play from off-stage.

Wendy Kesselman's dramatisation alters none of the original events: after years of faithful and scorned service, the main characters Christine and Lea violently murder Madame and Mademoiselle Danzard, cutting and tearing the bodies of their mistresses, smashing teeth and bone, removing the eye of one of their victims 'without the aid of an instrument'. From its first moment, the play explores the motivations for what seem inconceivable acts, arriving, by its courtroom conclusion, at a point where we understand the torture of constant condescension and may find these murders the only appropriate response.

My Sister in this House addresses almost every issue of consequence to feminist drama. The four women live together in a household that could breed affection and community, but class distinctions separate Madame and Mademoiselle Danzard from their 'maids'. Isolated from others by the cruelty, rigid rules and exhausting demands of their employers, Lea and Christine find their only solace in each other. Almost imperceptibly they come to be lovers. Genet's maids think of themselves as dirt, as the despicable residence of 'bad smells'. Kesselman's sisters like their own and each other's bodies; one of Christine's joys is in making her sister beautiful. Although Christine and Lea become sad and angry as they realise that their dream of escape to their own farm will never be possible on their meagre wages, they also become liberated from the illusion that Madame genuinely cares for them. In contrast, the self-hatred that Genet attributes to the maids not only makes his maids victims, but victims at their own hands.

In *The Maids* power resides in a man. *My Sister in this House* suggests that domination and the abuse of power corrupt, no matter what the biological sex of the player. Although *My Sister in this House* contains no male characters, it nevertheless depicts a world in which class and gender domination are inseparable. By emphasising evidence associated with documentary re-presentations of history – photographs, letters, courtroom testimony – Kesselman's play gives dramatic form to the knowledge that patriarchy is a social institution, carefully recorded but transparent only if properly framed. From its opening scene in which Lea and Christine appear as if posing for a photograph, the play suggests the human desire for accurate self-images and the inseparability of image and role from context.

Lea and Christine do not just murder, they assault the sources of their oppression. They do so out of a love that can no longer bear to see the other demeaned or in pain. If the records of events in 1933 do not support this motivation, a broader history of women does. History does not make murder acceptable but it does serve as a warning of the inevitability of violence in the absence of constructive and radical transformations in social structures. Kesselman's dramaturgy reminds us persistently that this is a moment in history, frozen in photographs and liberated by the mobility of theatre. Her play articulates an important distinction between social realism which reveals the underlying structures and institutions of a culture and conventional realism which describes the individual desires and manners of middle-class characters. In the latter, we are voyeurs, able to escape what we see without notice or effect; in the former we are witnesses, responsible to the history presented.

For more than fifteen years, feminist dramatists have been exploring that broader history, rethinking it and recreating it in plays that command our attention. In so doing, feminist drama has altered the course of theatre history. Juxtaposed to Genet's *The Maids*, Kesselman's *My Sister in this House* raises important questions about the nature of this change. Comparison of the two plays confirms the possibility of distinguishing between plays that are feminist and those that are not, and makes clear that subject matter is not the essential issue since the 'story' source for Genet and Kesselman is the same. It is what the playwright does with her or his material that matters – for feminist theatre and all theatre. Yet questions remain: is Kesselman's play *better* than Genet's or just more feminist? And, from the perspective of feminist drama, is this a legitimate question? Ancient questions of what we mean in the theatre by 'better' re-emerge. Can we judge the quality of a play, or at least the ability of a play to affect a contemporary audience, separate from the considerations raised by feminist playwrights?

A judgement of the relative value of Genet's and Kesselman's plays cannot and should not be arrived at by separating the theatrical merits of each from questions of feminism. If we think of feminist drama as primarily a thematic response to sociological issues, in the way in which abolition plays or plays about women's suffrage called attention to particular cultures or causes, then clearly the absence or presence of 'feminism' is irrelevant to basic judgements of theatrical quality. The persuasive argument in many of these plays, however, is that feminist drama presents a distinctive way of seeing and being in the world, not just a transient response to topical issues. For 2500 years, Western drama has derived much of its energy and asserted its place in society by envisioning the relationship between authority and sexuality. From the *Oresteia* to *Othello* to *Cloud Nine* and *My Sister in this House*, the power to act and the desire for erotic pleasure have been inseparably and relentlessly present on the stages of the theatre. The 'topic' is not new.

What is distinctive in feminist drama is the hints and glimpses it gives us of a form of theatre – and a form of life – in which authority and sexuality would no longer be primarily sources of *conflict.* For most of its history, theatre has given us the gift of knowing others and the inspiration to know ourselves. Feminist drama suggests that such gifts are valuable but insufficient, that for theatre to remain authentic it must offer not just recognition but images of individuals and relationships in the process of transformation. To accomplish this, it has not only turned away from conventional characterisations of women and men, but has celebrated on stage the ability of men and women to resist the roles that imprison them.

In its initial explorations, feminist drama has invited risk and challenged its audiences to have a similar courage to re-imagine itself as individuals and as a community. It is difficult to end this book because those risks continue and, in so doing, change the shape of the whole. Feminist drama aims to empower both the theatre and women. If it succeeds, then all theatre will address women and men from a 'feminist' perspective.

Notes

1. Roots and Contexts

1. Phyllis Mael, 'Interview with Honor Moore, Los Angeles, April 1978', in 'Catalog of Feminist Theater – Part I', *Chrysalis*, no. 10 (1979) p. 51.

2. Gertrude Stein, *Last Operas and Plays*, ed. Carl Van Vehten (New York: Vintage Books, 1978); 'Introduction' and 'Afterword' in *What Are Masterpieces?* (New York: Pitman, 1970) pp. viii, 98. This metaphor is also cited by Honor Moore in her 'Introduction' to *The New Women's Theatre* (New York: Vintage Books, 1977) p. xxv.

3. Patty Gillespie, 'Feminist Theatre', in Helen Chinoy and Linda Jenkins (eds), *Women in American Theater* (New York: Crown Publishers, 1981) p. 283.

4. See the description of this process as outlined by Meri Golden of the Alive and Trucking Theatre Company in Dinah Louise Leavitt, *Feminist Theatre Groups* (Jefferson, N.C.: McFarland, 1980) pp. 27–8.

5. Konstantin Stanislavsky, *My Life in Art*, trans. J. J. Robbins (New York: Theatre Arts Books, 1948) p. 143.

6. John Russell Taylor, *Anger and After*, paraphrase of Littlewood's remarks (London: Eyre Methuen, 1962) p. 120.

7. Sara Evans, *Personal Politics* (New York: Vintage Books, 1980) p. 86.

8. Charlotte Rea, 'Women's Theater Groups', *The Drama Review*, vol. 16, no. 2 (June 1972) p. 82.

9. Michelene Wandor, *Understudies* (London: Eyre Methuen, 1981) p. 32.

2. Foothills: Precursors of Feminist Drama

1. 'Rosa White', unpublished paper by Martha Stifler Waller.

2. Lorraine Hansberry, *A Raisin in the Sun*, in Lindsay Patterson (ed.), *Black Theatre* (New York: New American Library, 1971) p. 355.

3. Ibid., p. 374.

4. Interview with Joan Littlewood in *Behind the Scenes: Theater and Film Interviews from the Transatlantic Review* (New York: Holt, Rinehart & Winston, 1971) pp. 1–12.

5. John Russell Taylor, *Anger and After* (London: Eyre Methuen, 1962) p. 131.

6. Shelagh Delaney, *A Taste of Honey* (New York: Grove Press, 1959) p. 72.

7. Michelene Wandor, *Understudies* (London: Eyre Methuen, 1981) p. 75.

8. Helene Keyssar, 'I Love You, Who Are You: the Strategy of Drama in Recognition Scenes', *PMLA*, March 1977, pp. 297–306.

9. Shelagh Delaney, *The Lion in Love* (London: Eyre Methuen, 1961) p. 85.

10. Taylor, *Anger and After*, p. 77.

11. Ann Jellicoe, 'Preface' to *Sport of My Mad Mother*, rev. edn (London: Faber & Faber, 1964) p. 5.

12. Doris Lessing, letter to the author, March 1982.

3. Megan Terry: Mother of American Feminist Drama

1. Dinah L. Leavitt, 'Megan Terry', interview in Helen Chinoy and Linda Jenkins (eds), *Women in American Theater* (New York: Crown Publishers, 1981) p. 288.

2. Megan Terry, interview with the author, January 1982, Omaha, Nebraska.

3. Viola Spolin's *Improvisation for the Theatre* (New York: Pitman, 1965) was a bible for transformational training in the sixties and seventies.

4. Megan Terry, *Hothouse* (New York: Samuel French, 1975).

5. Megan Terry, *Keep Tightly Closed in a Cool Dry Place*, in *Four Plays by Megan Terry* (New York: Simon & Schuster, 1967) p. 6.

6. Megan Terry, *Calm Down Mother*, in Victoria Sullivan and James Hatch (eds), *Plays By and About Women* (New York: Vintage Books, 1973) p. 279.

7. Megan Terry, interview with Phyllis Jane Wagner, 4 March 1972, cited in 'Introduction', *Approaching Simone* (New York: The Feminist Press, 1973) p. 13.

8. Jo-Ann Schmidman and Megan Terry, in an interview with the author, January 1982, Omaha, Nebraska.

9. Ibid.

10. Ibid.

4. The Dramas of Caryl Churchill

1. C. W. E. Bigsby, *Contemporary English Drama* (London: Edward Arnold, 1981) pp. 13–18.

2. Catherine Itzin, *Stages of the Revolution* (London: Eyre Methuen, 1980) p. 281.

3. Ibid., p. 279.

4. Caryl Churchill, in an interview with the author, March 1982.

5. Ibid. Unless specifically stated, all quotes from Caryl Churchill come from the author's interview.

6. Itzin, *Stages of the Revolution*, p. 282.

7. Michelene Wandor, *Understudies* (London: Methuen, 1981) p. 66.

8. Itzin, *Stages of the Revolution*, p. 221.

9. Caryl Churchill, 'A Note on the Production', in *Light Shining in Buckinghamshire* (London: Pluto Plays, 1978).

10. Ibid.

11. Michael Goldman, *The Actor's Freedom* (New York: Viking Press, 1975).

12. Dorothy Dinnerstein, *The Mermaid and the Minotaur* (New York: Harper & Row, 1976) p. 161.

13. Michelene Wandor (ed.), *Plays by Women* (London: Methuen, 1982) vol. 1, p. 39.

14. Caryl Churchill, 'If You Float', in *Vinegar Tom* (London: TQ Publications, 1978).

5. A Network of Playwrights

1. Vivian Gornick and Barbara K. Moran, *Women in Sexist Society* (New York: A Mentor Book, New American Library, 1971) p. 40.

2. Myrna Lamb, *The Mod Donna and Scyklon Z* (New York: Pathfinder Press, 1971) p. 28.

3. Adrienne Kennedy, *Funnyhouse of a Negro*, in William Brasmer and Dominick Consolo (eds), *Black Drama* (Columbus, Ohio: Charles E. Merrill, 1970) p. 258.

4. Rochelle Owens, *Futz*, in Albert Poland and Bruce Mailman (eds), *The Off-Off-Broadway Book* (New York: Bobbs-Merrill, 1972) p. 198.

5. Rosalyn Drexler, *Skywriting*, in Rachel France (ed.), *A Century of Plays by American Women* (New York: Richards Rosen Press, 1979) p. 177.

6. Honor Moore, 'Introduction' to *The New Women's Theatre* (New York: Vintage Books, 1977). I want to thank Moore here for valuable research and information that persistently informs this book.

7. Tina Howe, *Birth and After Birth*, in Honor Moore (ed.), *New Women's Theatre* (New York: Vintage Books, 1977) p. 129.

8. Honor Moore, *Mourning Pictures*, in Honor Moore (ed.), *New Women's Theatre*, p. 235.

9. Maria Irene Fornes, *Fefu and Her Friends*, in *Performing Arts Journal*, Winter 1978, pp. 116–17.

6. Communities of Women in Drama

1. Pam Gems, 'Interview' with Ann McFerrans, *Time Out*, 21–7 October 1977; quoted in Michelene Wandor, *Understudies* (London: Eyre Methuen, 1981) p. 63.

2. Pam Gems, in Michelene Wandor (ed.), *Plays by Women* (London: Methuen, 1982) vol. 1, pp. 72–3.

3. Pam Gems, *Dusa, Fish, Stas and Vi*, in Wandor (ed.), ibid., vol. 1, p. 70.

4. Michelene Wandor, 'Introduction' to *Strike While the Iron is Hot* (London: Journeyman Press, 1980) p. 11.

5. Commentary by Kate Crutchley and Nancy Duiguid, in ibid., p. 63.

6. Commentary by Michelene Wandor on *Aurora Leigh*, in Wandor (ed.), *Plays for Women*, vol. 1, p. 134.

7. Michelene Wandor, *Aurora Leigh*, in ibid., p. 107.

8. Ntozake Shange, *Three Pieces* (New York: Penguin Books, 1982) p. ix.

9. Ibid., p. xii.

10. Ibid., pp. xii–xiii.

11. Some of this material draws upon commentary on *for colored girls* in my previously published book *The Curtain and the Veil: Strategies in Black Drama* (New York: Burt Franklin, 1982) pp. 212–17.

12. Ntozake Shange, *for colored girls* (New York: Macmillan, 1975) p. 11.

13. Ibid., p. 35.

14. Ibid., p. 60.

15. Shange, *Three Pieces*, p. 113.

16. Ibid., p. 117.

7. Success and its Limits

1. Wendy Wasserstein, *Uncommon Women and Others* (New York: Avon Books, 1978) p. 74.

2. Mel Gussow, 'New Voices in the Theater', *New York Times Magazine*, 1 May 1983, p. 40.

8. Nooks, Crannies and New Directions

1. Chris Rawlence, 'Introduction' to *Strike While the Iron is Hot*, in Michelene Wandor (ed.), *Strike While the Iron is Hot* (London: Journeyman Press, 1980) p. 19.

2. Mica Nava, 'Introduction' to *My Mother Says I Never Should*, in ibid., pp. 115–16.

3. The Women's Theatre Group, *My Mother Says I Never Should*, in ibid., p. 141.

4. Martha Boesing in collaboration with At the Foot of the Mountain, *The Story of a Mother, A Ritual*, in Helen Chinoy and Linda Jenkins (eds), *Women in American Theater* (New York: Crown Publishers, 1981) p. 44.

5. I wish to thank Angela Didio who reported to me on the Festival.

6. William M. Hoffman (ed.), *Gay Plays* (New York: Avon Books, 1979) pp. ix–x.

Bibliography

Where information was available, place and date of first productions are noted. In many instances some plays were subsequently produced in other locations. In other instances plays listed here have been produced but date and locations were unavailable.

Akalaitas, Joanne, *Dead End Kids: A History of Nuclear Power* (produced at Mabou Mines, New York, 1980).
Boesing, Martha, *Accent of Fools* (First Play, at Connecticut College for Women).
——, *The Wanderer* (produced at Minneapolis Opera Co., Minneapolis, 1969).
——, *Earth Song* (produced by American Friends Service Committee, 1970).
——, *Pimp* (produced by At the Foot of the Mountain, Minneapolis, 1973).
——, *The Gelding* (produced by At the Foot of the Mountain, Minneapolis, 1974). In collaboration with At the Foot of the Mountain.
——, *Raped: A Woman's Look at Brecht's Exception and the Rule* (produced by At the Foot of the Mountain, Minneapolis, 1976). In collaboration with At the Foot of the Mountain.
——, *Mad Emma* (1977).

——, *The Moon Tree* (produced by At the Foot of the Mountain, Minneapolis, 1977).

——, *Journeys Along the Matrix: Three Plays by Martha Boesing* (includes *The Gelding, River Journal, Love Song for an Amazon*) (Minneapolis: Vanilla Press, 1978).

Bovasso, Julie, *The Moon Dreamers* (also director: produced New York, 1967; rev. version, New York, 1969) (New York: Samuel French, 1972).

——, *Gloria and Esperanza* (also director: produced New York, 1968; rev. version, New York, 1970) (New York: Samuel French, 1973).

——, *Schubert's Last Serenade* (produced New York, 1971), in *Spontaneous Combustion: Eight New American Plays*, ed. Rochelle Owens (New York: Winter House, 1972).

——, *Monday on the Way to Mercury Island* (produced New York, 1971).

——, *Down by the River Where Waterlilies Are Disfigured Every Day* (produced Providence, Rhode Island, 1972; New York, 1975).

——, *The Nothing Kid, and Standard Safety* (also director: produced New York, 1974); *Standard Safety* (New York: Samuel French, 1976).

——, *Super Lover, Schubert's Serenade, and the Final Analysis* (also director: produced New York, 1975).

Chambers, Jane, *Tales of the Revolution and Other American Fables* (produced at Eugene O'Neill Theater, Waterford, Conn.).

——, *Random Violence* (produced at the Women's Interart Theatre, New York City).

——, *One Short Day at the Jamboree* (produced at Town Hall, New York City).

——, *Curfew!* (New York: WNYC-TV).

——, *Mine!* (produced at the Women's Interart Theatre, New York City).

——, *The Wife* (produced at the Women's Interart Theatre, New York City).

——, *A Late Snow*; in *Gay Plays: The First Collection*, ed. William Hoffman (New York: Avon Books, 1979).

——, *Common Garden Variety* (produced at Mark Taper Lab, Office for Advanced Drama Research, Los Angeles, California, 1976).

192

Bibliography

——, *Eye of the Gull* (manuscript).

——, *Deadly Nightshade* (manuscript).

——, *Last Summer at Bluefish Cove* (New York: The Glines).

——, *My Blue Heaven* (manuscript).

——, *Kudzu* (manuscript).

Childress, Alice, *Florence*, in *Masses and Midstream* (New York, October 1950).

——, *Trouble in Mind* (produced New York, 1955), in *Black Theatre: A Twentieth-Century Collection of the Work of Its Best Playwrights*, ed. Lindsay Patterson (New York: Dodd Mead, 1971).

——, *Wedding Band* (produced Ann Arbor, Michigan, 1966; New York, 1972) (New York: Samuel French, 1973).

——, *The World on a Hill*, in *Plays to Remember* (New York: Macmillan, 1968).

——, *String* (produced New York, 1969), in *Mojo, and String* (New York: Dramatists Play Service, 1971).

——, *Wine in the Wilderness* (televised 1969) (New York: Dramatists Play Service, 1970).

——, *Mojo, and String* (New York: Dramatists Play Service, 1971).

——, *When the Rattlesnake Sounds* (juvenile) (New York: Coward McCann, 1975).

——, *Let's Hear It for the Queen* (juvenile) (New York: Coward McCann, 1976).

Churchill, Caryl, *Downstairs* (produced Oxford, 1958; London, 1959).

——, *Having a Wonderful Time* (produced London, 1960).

——, *Easy Death* (produced Oxford, 1962).

——, *The Ants* (broadcast, 1962), in *Penguin New English Dramatists 12* (Harmondsworth: Penguin, 1968).

——, *Lovesick* (radio play, London, 1966).

——, *Identical Twins* (radio play, London, 1968).

——, *Abortive* (radio play, London, 1971).

——, *Not . . . Not . . . Not Enough Oxygen* (radio play, London, 1971).

——, *Schreber's Nervous Illness* (broadcast, 1972; produced London, 1972).

——, *Henry's Past* (radio play, London, 1972).

——, *The Judge's Wife* (television play, London, 1972).

——, *Owners* (produced London, 1972; New York, 1973) (London: Eyre Methuen, 1973).

——, *Perfect Happiness* (broadcast, 1973; produced London, 1974).

——, *Turkish Delight* (television play, London, 1974).

——, *Eleventh Hour* (television play, London, 1975).

——, *Moving Clocks Go Slow* (produced London, 1975).

——, *Objections to Sex and Violence* (produced London, 1975).

——, *Light Shining in Buckinghamshire* (produced London, 1976) (London: Pluto Press, 1978).

——, *Traps* (produced London, 1976) (London: Pluto Press, 1977).

——, *Vinegar Tom* (produced London, 1976 and Northampton, 1979) (London: TQ Publications, 1978).

——, *Floorshow* (produced London, 1977).

——, *The After Dinner Joke* (television play, London, 1978).

——, *The Legion Hall Bombing* (television play, London, 1978).

——, *Cloud Nine* (produced London, 1979 and New York, 1980) (London: Pluto Press, 1979).

——, *Three More Sleepless Nights* (produced London, 1980).

——, *Top Girls* (produced London, 1982; New York, 1983) (London: Methuen, 1983).

——, *Fen* (produced London, 1983; New York, 1983) (London: Methuen, 1983).

Delaney, Shelagh, *A Taste of Honey* (produced London, 1958; New York, 1960) (London: Methuen, 1959; New York: Grove Press, 1959).

——, *The Lion in Love* (produced Coventry and London, 1960; New York, 1963) (London: Eyre Methuen, 1961; New York: Grove Press, 1961).

——, *A Taste of Honey* (screenplay with Tony Richardson, New York, 1962).

——, *Sweetly Sings the Donkey* (New York: Putnam, 1963; London: Methuen, 1964).

——, *The White Bus* (screenplay, New York, 1966).

——, *Charley Bubbles* (screenplay, New York, 1968).

——, *Did Your Nanny Come from Bergen?* (television play, New York, 1970).

——, *St. Martin's Summer* (television play, New York, 1974).

Drexler, Rosalyn, *The Line of Least Existence and Other Plays: Home Movies* (produced New York, 1964); *The Investigation* (produced Boston and New York, 1966); *Hot Buttered Roll* (produced New York, 1966; London, 1970); *Softly* (produced New York, 1964); *Consider the Nearness* (produced New York, 1964); *The Bed Was Full* (produced New York, 1972) (New York: Random House, 1967).

——, *Skywriting* (produced New York, 1968); published in *Collision Course* (New York: Random House, 1968).

——, *She Who Was He* (produced Virginia Commonwealth University, Richmond, 1974).

——, *Travesty Parade* (produced Center Theatre Group, Los Angeles, California, 1974).

——, *Vulgar Lives* (produced Theatre Strategy, New York, 1979).

——, *Writer's Opera* (produced Theatre for the New City, New York, 1979).

——, *Starburn and the Story of Jenni Love* (1980).

Duffy, Maureen, *Josie* (television play, London, 1961).

——, *The Lay Off* (produced London, 1962).

——, *The Silk Room* (produced Watford, Herts, 1966).

——, *Rites* (produced London, 1969) (London: Methuen, 1969).

——, *Solo, Olde Tyme* (produced Cambridge, 1970).

——, *A Nightingale in Bloomsbury Square* (produced London, 1973); in *Factions*, ed. Giles Gordon and Alex Hamilton (London, 1974).

Dunn, Nell, *Up the Junction* (London: MacGibon & Kee, 1963).

——, *Talking to Women* (London: MacGibon & Kee, 1965).

——, *Poor Cow*, 1st edn (Garden City, New York: Doubleday, 1967).

——, *The Incurable*, 1st edn (Garden City, New York: Double-day, 1971).

——, *Steaming* (produced London, 1981–2; New York, 1982–3) (Ambergate, Derbyshire: Amber Lane Press, 1981).

Dunn, Nell and Adrian Henri, *I Want* (London: Jonathan Cape, 1972).

Fornes, Maria Irene, *The Widow* (produced New York, 1961); published as *La Viuda*, in *Cuatro Autores Cubanos* (Havana: Casa de las Americas, 1961).

——, *Tango Palace* (as *There! You Died*, produced San Francisco, Actors' Workshop, 1963; as *Tango Palace*, produced New

York, 1964; rev. version, also director: produced Minneapolis, 1965); in *Promenade and Other Plays* (New York: Winter House, 1971).

——, *The Successful Life of Three: A Skit for Vauderville* (produced Finehouse Theatre, Minneapolis, and Open Theatre, New York, 1965); in *Promenade and Other Plays* (New York: Winter House, 1971).

——, *Promenade*, music by Al Carmines (produced Judson Church, New York, 1965); in *Promenade and Other Plays* (New York: Winter House, 1971).

——, *The Office* (produced New York, 1966).

——, *A Vietnamese Wedding* (produced Washington Square Church, New York, 1967); in *Promenade and Other Plays* (New York: Winter House, 1971).

——, *The Annunciation* (also director: produced Judson Church, New York, 1967).

——, *Dr. Kheal* (produced Village Gate, New York, 1968; London, 1969); in *Promenade and Other Plays* (New York: Winter House, 1971).

——, *The Red Burning Light; or, Mission XQ3* (produced Zurich, 1968; Open Theatre, New York, 1969); in *Promenade and Other Plays* (New York: Winter House, 1971).

——, *Molly's Dream* (produced Lenox, Mass., 1968; also director: produced New York, 1968); in *Promenade and Other Plays* (New York: Winter House, 1971).

——, *The Curse of the Langston House* (produced Cincinnati Playhouse, OH).

——, *Promenade and Other Plays* (includes *A Vietnamese Wedding*, *The Red Burning Light; or, Mission XQ3*, *Dr. Kheal*, *Molly's Dream*, *Tango Palace*, *The Successful Life of Three*) (New York: Winter House, 1971).

——, *Baboon!!!*, with others (produced Cincinnati, 1972).

——, *Aurora*, music by John FitzGibbon (also director: produced New York Theatre Strategy, New York, 1974).

——, *Eyes of Harem* (produced Intar Theatre, New York).

——, *Cap-a-Pie*, music by Jose Raul Bernardo (also director: produced New York, 1975).

——, *Fefu and her Friends* (produced New York, 1977), in *Performing Arts Journal*, Winter 1978, pp. 112–70.

——, *Evelyn Brown (A Diary)* (produced Theater for the New City, New York).

Bibliography

Franceschild, Donna, *The President is Dead* (produced Pepperbad Co , Los Angeles, California, 1971).

——, *A Nice Day* (produced University of California at Los Angeles, 1972).

——, *The Strange Little Man in the Garbage Can* (produced University of California at Los Angeles, 1972).

——, *The Triple Decker Drama of the Historical Battle of Captain Kangeroo and the Children's Crusade vs. the Lionheart Legion vs. the Commie Meanies* (produced University of California at Los Angeles, 1973).

——, *The Committee Investigation into the Spread of Discontent at the George Saxon Souvenir Co.* (produced University of California at Los Angeles, 1974).

——, *The Secret Story of the Bit Players of Act II Scene 23* (produced Group Repertory Co., North Hollywood, California, 1975).

——, *Mutiny on the M1* (produced The Combination at the Albany Empire, 1980).

——, *Diaries* (produced Avon Touring Theatre Co., 1979).

——, *The Soap Opera* (produced Women's Theatre Group, London, 1979).

——, *Songs for Stray Cats and Other Living Creatures* (produced Cambridge Theatre Co., England, 1980–1).

——, *Tap Dance on a Telephone Line* (produced Action Space, 1981).

——, *The Cleaning Lady* (produced Soho Poly, London, 1977).

Gems, Pam, *Betty's Wonderful Christmas* (produced Cockpit Theatre, 1972).

——, *My Warren, After Birthday* (produced Almost Free Theatre, 1973).

——, *The Amiable Courtship of Miz Venus and Wild Bill* (produced Almost Free Theatre, 1974).

——, *Go West, Young Woman* (produced Roundhouse, 1974).

——, *Up in Sweden* (produced Haymarket, Leicester, 1975).

——, *My Name is Rosa Luxembourg* translation from Marianne Auricoste (produced Soho Poly, London 1976).

——, *The Rivers and Forests*, trans. from Duras (produced Soho Poly, London, 1976).

——, *The Project* (produced Soho Poly, London, 1976).

——, *Guinevere* (Edinburgh Festival, 1976).

——, *Dusa, Fish, Stas and Vi* (produced London, Edinburgh Festival, 1976) (New York: Samuel French, 1977).

——, *Queen Christina* (produced Royal Shakespeare Company, The Other Place, 1977).

——, *Piaf* (produced Royal Shakespeare Co., The Other Place, 1978) (New York: Samuel French, 1979).

——, *Uncle Vanya*, new version of Chekhov play (produced Hampstead Theatre Club, 1979).

——, *A Doll's House*, new version of the play by Ibsen (produced Tyne and Wear, 1980).

Gooch, Steve, *The NAB Show* (produced Brighton, 1970).

——, *Great Expectations*, adaptation of a novel by Charles Dickens (produced Liverpool, 1970).

——, *Man Is Man*, adaptation of the play by Bertolt Brecht (produced London, 1971).

——, *It's All for the Best*, adaptation of the novel *Candide* by Voltaire (produced Stoke-on-Trent, 1972).

——, *Big Wolf*, adaptation of a play by Harald Mueller (produced London, 1972) (London: Davis Poynter, 1972).

——, *Will Wat; If Not, What Will?* (produced London, 1972) (London: Pluto Press, 1975).

——, *Prison* (produced Exeter, 1972).

——, *The Mother*, adaptation of the play by Bertolt Brecht (produced London, 1973).

——, *Female Transport* (produced London, 1973; New York, 1976) (London: Pluto Press, 1975).

——, *Dick* (produced London, 1973).

——, *The Motor Show*, with Paul Thompson (produced Dagenham, Essex, and London, 1974) (London: Pluto Press, 1975).

——, *Cock-Artist*, adaptation of the play by R. W. Fassbinder (produced London, 1974).

——, *Strike '26*, with Frank McDermott (produced London, 1975).

——, *Made in Britain*, with Paul Thompson (produced Oxford, 1976).

——, *Our Land, Our Lives* (produced London, 1976).

——, *Nicked* (1972).

——, *Back-Street Romeo.*

Griffin, Susan, *Dear Sky* (San Lorenzo, California: Shameless Hussy Press, 1971).

Bibliography

——, *Le Viol* (L'Etincelle, Canada, 1972).

——, *Let Them Be Said* (Ma Ma Press, 1973).

——, *Letters* (Twowindows Press, 1974).

——, *The Sink* (San Lorenzo, California: Shameless Hussy Press, 1974).

——, *Voices: A Play* (New York: Feminist Press, 1975).

——, *Like the Iris of an Eye* (New York: Harper & Row, 1976).

——, *Woman and Nature: The Roaring Inside Her* (produced 1978).

——, *Rape: The Power of Consciousness* (New York: Harper & Row, 1979).

Hansberry, Lorraine, *A Raisin in the Sun* (produced New York and London, 1959) (New York: Random House, 1959; London: Methuen, 1960).

——, *The Sign in Sidney Brustein's Window* (produced New York, 1964) (New York: Random House, 1965); in *Three Negro Plays* (London: Penguin, 1969).

——, *Les Blancs*, ed. Robert Nemiroff (produced New York, 1970); in *The Collected Last Plays of Lorraine Hansberry*, ed., Robert Nemiroff (New York: Random House, 1972).

——, *Les Blancs: The Collected Last Plays of Lorraine Hansberry* (includes *Les Blancs*, *The Drinking Gourd*, *What Use Are Flowers?*), ed. Robert Nemiroff (New York: Random House, 1972).

Hellman, Lillian, *The Children's Hour* (produced New York, 1934; London, 1936) (New York: Knopf, 1934; London: Hamish Hamilton, 1937). Also reprinted in various anthologies.

——, *Days to Come* (produced New York, 1936) (New York and London: Knopf, 1936).

——, *The Little Foxes* (produced New York, 1939; Sutton Coldfield, Warwickshire, 1946) (New York: Random House, 1939; London: Hamish Hamilton, 1939). Also reprinted in various anthologies.

——, *Watch on the Rhine* (produced New York, 1941; London, 1942) (New York: Random House, 1941; London, English Theatre Guild, 1946).

——, *Four Plays* (includes *The Children's Hour*, *Days to Come*, *The Little Foxes* and *Watch on the Rhine*) (New York: Random House, 1942).

——, *The North Star: A Motion Picture about Some Russian People* (New York: Viking Press, 1943).

——, *The Searching Wind* (produced New York, 1944) (New York: Viking Press, 1944); in *Collected Plays* (1972).

——, *Another Part of the Forest* (also director: produced New York, 1946; Liverpool, 1953) (New York: Viking Press, 1947); in *Collected Plays* (1972).

——, *Montserrat*, adaptation of the play by Emmanuel Robles (also director: produced New York, 1949; London, 1954) (New York: Dramatists Play Service, 1950); in *Collected Plays* (1972).

——, *Regina*, music by Marc Blitztein (produced New York, 1949).

——, *The Autumn Garden* (produced New York, 1951) (Boston, Mass.: Little, Brown, 1951); in *Collected Plays* (1972).

——, *The Lark*, adaptation of the play by Jean Anouilh (produced New York, 1955) (New York: Random House, 1955); in *Collected Plays* (1972).

——, *Candide*, music by Leonard Bernstein, lyrics by Richard Wilbur, John LaTouche and Dorothy Parker, adaptation of the novel by Voltaire (produced New York, 1956; London, 1959) (New York: Random House, 1957); in *Collected Plays* (1972).

——, *Toys in the Attic* (produced New York and London, 1960) (New York, Random House, 1960); in *Collected Plays* (1972).

——, *Six Plays* (New York: Modern Library, 1960).

——, *My Mother, My Father and Me*, adaptation of the novel *How Much?* by Burt Blechman (produced New York, 1963) (New York: Random House, 1963); in *Collected Plays* (1972).

——, *The Collected Plays of Lillian Hellman* (includes *The Children's Hour*, *Days to Come*, *The Little Foxes*, *Watch on the Rhine*, *The Searching Wind*, *Another Part of the Forest*, *Montserrat*, *The Autumn Garden*, *The Lark*, *Candide*, *Toys in the Attic*, *My Mother, My Father and Me*) (Boston, Mass.: Little, Brown, 1972; London: Macmillan, 1972).

Henley, Beth, *Crimes of the Heart* (produced Actors Theatre of Louisville, Kentucky, 1979; Golden Theatre, New York, 1981) (New York: Dramatists Play Service, 1982).

——, *Am I Blue* (produced by Circle Repertory Theatre, New York, 1982).

——, *The Wake of Jimmy Foster* (produced off-Broadway, New York, 1981).

Bibliography

——, *The Miss Firecracker Contest* (produced Manhattan Theatre, New York, 1984).

Holden, Joan (S.F. Mime Troupe), *The Independent Female or A Man Has His Pride* (produced San Francisco Mime Troupe, San Francisco, 1970); in *A Century of Plays by American Women*, ed. Rachel France (New York: Richards Rosen Press, 1979).

Howe, Tina, *The Nest* (produced Act IV Theater, Provincetown, MA and Mercury Theatre, New York, 1970).

——, *Birth and After Birth* (produced New Women's Theatre, Gotham Arts Theater, New York, 1974); in *The New Women's Theater*, ed. Honor Moore (New York: Vintage Books, 1977).

——, *Museum* (produced Los Angeles Actors Theater, Los Angeles, and New York, 1976) (New York: Samuel French, 1977).

——, *Painting Churches* (produced Second Stage, New York, 1983).

——, *The Art of Dining* (produced New York Shakespeare Festival, New York, and Kennedy Center, Washington, D.C.) (New York: Samuel French).

Jacker, Corinne, *Later* (produced Phoenix Theatre, New York) (New York: Dramatists Play Service, 1975).

——, *Harry Outside: A Play in Two Acts* (produced O'Neill Theatre Center's National Playwriters Conference, CT; Circle Repertory Co., New York) (New York: Dramatists Play Service, 1975).

——, *Bits and Pieces* (produced Manhattan Theatre Club, New York; E.P. Conkle Workshop, Dallas, TX) (New York: Dramatists Play Service).

——, *Breakfast, Lunch and Dinner* (produced Actors Studio, New York; E.P. Conkle Workshop, Dallas, TX).

——, *Travellers* (produced O'Neill Theater Center's National Playwrights Conference, CT; Cincinnati Playhouse-in-the-Park, OH).

——, *Making It* (produced Circle Repertory Company, New York).

——, *Night Thoughts* (produced Circle Repertory Company, New York) (New York: Dramatists Play Service).

——, *Terminal* (produced Circle Repertory Company, New York).

——, *My Life* (produced Circle Repertory Company, New York) (New York: Dramatists Play Service).

——, *The Other People's Table* (produced Billy Munk Theatre, New York).

——, *Chinese Restaurant Syndrome* (produced Billy Munk Theatre, New York); in *Best Short Plays of 1979* (Radnor, PA: Chilton Press, 1979).

——, *After the Season* (produced American Festival Theatre, Lake Forest, IL).

——, *Domestic Issues* (produced Yale Repertory, CT).

Jellicoe, Ann, *Rosmersholm*, adaptation of the play by Ibsen (also director: produced London, 1952; rev. version, produced London, 1959) (San Francisco: Chandler, 1960).

——, *The Lady from the Sea*, adaptation of the play by Ibsen (produced London, 1961).

——, *The Knack* (also co-director: produced Cambridge, 1961; London, 1962; Boston, 1963; New York, 1964) (London: Encore, 1962; New York: Samuel French, 1962).

——, *The Sport of My Mad Mother* (also co-director: produced London, 1958); published in *The Observer Plays* (London: Faber, 1958; rev. version, London: Faber, 1964); in *Two Plays* (1964).

——, *The Seagull*, with Ariadne Nicolaeff, adaptation of the play by Chekhov (produced London, 1964).

——, *Der Freischutz*, translation of the libretto by Friedrich Kind, music by Weber (produced London, 1964).

——, *Two Plays: The Knack and The Sport of My Mad Mother* (New York: Dell, 1964).

——, *Shelley: or, The Idealist* (also director: produced London, 1965) (London: Faber, 1966; New York: Grove Press, 1966).

——, *The Rising Generation* (produced London, 1967); published in *Playbill 2*, ed. Alan Durband (London: Hutchinson, 1969).

——, *The Giveaway* (produced Edinburgh, 1968; London, 1969) (London: Faber, 1970).

——, *You'll Never Guess* (also director: produced London, 1973); in *3 Jelliplays* (1975).

——, *Two Jelliplays: Clever Elsie, Smiling Jack, Silent Peter and A Good Thing and a Bad Thing* (also director: produced London, 1974); in *3 Jelliplays* (1975).

——, *3 Jelliplays* (includes *You'll Never Guess*; *Clever Elsie, Smiling Jack, Silent Peter*; *A Good Thing and a Bad Thing*) (London: Faber, 1975).

Bibliography

Kennedy, Adrienne, *The Lennon Play: In His Own Write*, with John Lennon and Victor Spinetti, adaptation of works by John Lennon (produced London, 1967; rev. version, produced London, 1968) (London: Jonathan Cape, 1968).

——, *A Lesson in Dead Language* (produced New York and London, 1968); in *Collision Course* (New York: Random House, 1968).

——, *A Rat's Mass* (produced New York and London, 1970); in *New Black Playwrights*, ed. William Couch, Jr. (Baton Rouge: Louisiana State University Press, 1968).

——, *A Beast's Story* (produced New York, 1965); in *Cities in Bezique* (1969).

——, *The Owl Answers* (produced Westport, Connecticut, and New York, 1965); in *Cities in Bezique* (1969).

——, *Funnyhouse of a Negro* (produced New York, 1964; London, 1968) (New York: Samuel French, 1969).

——, *Boats* (produced Los Angeles, 1969).

——, *Sun: A Poem for Malcolm X Inspired by His Murder* (produced London, 1969); in *Scripts 1* (New York: November 1971).

——, *Cities of Bezique: 2 One-Act Plays: The Owl Answer and A Beast's Story* (New York: Samuel French, 1969).

——, *An Evening with Dead Essex* (produced New York, 1973).

Kesselman, Wendy, *My Sister in this House* (produced Second Stage, New York, 1981–2).

Lamb, Myrna, *The Serving Girl and the Lady* (produced NFRPT, Martinique Theater; Village Gate, New York).

——, *But What Have You Done for Me Lately?* (produced NFRPT, Washington Square Church, New York).

——, *The Butcher Shop*, in *Aphra*, vol. 1, no. 2, Winter 1970, pp. 28–32.

——, *In the Shadow of the Crematorium* (produced New Feminist Repertory Theatre, New York).

——, *I Lost a Pair of Gloves Yesterday* (produced Manhattan Theater Club, New York, and One Act Theater Co., Berkeley, CA).

——, *The Mod Donna and Scyklon Z: Plays of Women Liberation*; includes *But What Have You Done for Me Lately?*; *Monologia*; *Pas de Deux*; *The Butcher Shop*; *The Serving Girl and the Lady*; *In the Shadow of the Crematorium* (New York: Pathfinder Press, 1971).

203

——, *Apple Pie* (produced New York Shakespeare Festival Theatre, New York, and Center for Theater Research, Buffalo, NY).

——, *Jillila* (manuscript).

——, *Crab Quadrille* (produced Interart Theatre, New York).

——, *The Sacrifice* (produced AMDA Theater, New York).

——, *Olympic Park* (produced New York Shakespeare Festival, New York).

——, *Ballad of Brooklyn* (produced Brooklyn Academy, New York).

——, *The Comeback Act* (produced Interart Theatre, New York).

——, *Mother Ann* (New York).

——, *The Two Party System* (produced Interart Theatre, New York).

Lauro, Shirley, *The Contest* (produced Alley Theater, Houston, 1976).

——, *The Story of Margaret/The Story of Kit*.

——, *Lessons*; includes *I Don't Know Where You're Coming From At All*; *Open Admissions*; *Nothing Immediate* (New York).

Lessing, Doris, *Mr. Dolinger* (1958).

——, *Each In His Own Wilderness*, in *New English Dramatists: Three Plays*, ed. by Elliot M. Browne (Harmondsworth: Penguin, 1959) pp. 11–95.

——, *The Truth About Billy Newton* (1960).

——, *Play with a Tiger: A Play in Three Acts* (London: Michael Joseph, 1962).

Littlewood, Joan, *Oh What a Lovely War* (produced Broadhurst Theater, New York, 1965).

Lowe, Stephen, *Comic Pictures* (produced Scarborough, 1976).

——, *Sally Ann Hallelujah Band* (produced Nottingham, 1976).

——, *Touched* (produced Nottingham, 1981); in *Plays and Players* (London: Woodhouse Books, 1978; Eyre Methuen, 1981).

——, *Shooting Fishing and Riding* (produced Scarborough, 1977).

——, *Ragged Trousered Philanthropists* (produced Joint Stock, 1978).

——, *Cries from a Watchtower* (BBC1 television play, October 1979).

——, *Glasshouses* (produced London, 1981).

——, *Tibetan Inroads* (produced London, 1981) (London: Methuen, 1981).

——, *Shades* (BBC1 television play, 1982).

Malpede, Karen, *Three Works by the Open Theatre* (New York: Drama Book Specialists, 1974).

——, *Rebeccah* (New York: Playwrights Horizon, 1975).

——, *The End of War* (produced New Cycle Theatre, New York, 1977).

Martin, Jane, *Talking With* (produced Manhattan Theater Club, New York, 1982).

McCullers, Carson, *The Heart is a Lonely Hunter* (1940; film version, 1968).

——, *Reflections in a Golden Eye* (1941; film version, 1967).

——, *The Member of the Wedding* (1946; dramatisation, 1951; film version, 1952) (New York: New Directions, 1951).

——, *The Ballad of the Sad Cafe* (1951; dramatisation by E. Albee, 1963).

——, *The Square Root of Wonderful* (1958).

——, *Clock Without Hands* (1961).

——, *Sweet As a Pickle and Clean As a Pig: Poems* (1964).

——, *The Mortgaged Heart*, ed. M. G. Smith (1971).

Merriam, Eve, *A Husband's Notes About Her* (New York: Collier Books, 1976).

——, *The Club* (New York: Samuel French, 1976).

——, *Out of Our Father's House*, in *The New Women's Theatre*, ed. Honor Moore (New York: Vintage Books, 1977).

Miller, Susan, *No One is Exactly Twenty-three*, in *Pyramid Magazine*, no. 1 (1968).

——, *Daddy/A Commotion of Zebras* (produced Alice Theatre, New York, 1970).

——, *Denim Lecture* (produced Mark Taper Forum Lab Theatre, Los Angeles; Pennsylvania State University, PA).

——, *Silverstein and Co* (produced Shakespeare Festival (Reading) New York).

——, *Confessions of a Female Disorder* (produced O'Neill Theatre Center's National Playwrite Conference, CT; Mark Taper Forum, New Theatre for Now, Los Angeles, CA); in *Gay Plays, First Collection*, ed. William Hoffman (New York: Avon Books, 1979).

——, *Flux* (produced New Phoenix Repertory Company, New York, and by the American Repertory Theatre, London, 1975).

——, *Cross Country*, in *West Coast Plays*, vol. 1 (Berkeley, California, 1975–6).

——, *Nasty Rumors and Final Remarks* (produced New York Shakespeare Festival, New York).

Moore, Honor, *Mourning Pictures* (produced Lenox Arts Center, MA); in *The New Women's Theatre: Ten Plays by Contemporary Women*, ed. Honor Moore (New York: Vintage Books, 1977).

——, *Years* (produced American Place Theatre, New York).

——, *The Terry Project* (with Victoria Rue) (manuscript).

Mueller, Lavonne, *Little Victories* (produced American Place Theatre, 1983).

Murray, Melissa, *Bouncing Back with Benyo* (co-written with Eileen Fairweather, produced Pirate Jenny tour, 1977).

——, *Hot Spot* (produced Women's Theatre Group, London, 1978).

——, *Belisha Beacon* (co-written with Eileen Fairweather, produced Pirate Jenny tour, 1978).

——, *Hormone Imbalance Revue* (also director: produced King's Head, Oval, 1979).

——, *Ophelia* (produced Hormone Imbalance at Action Space, London, 1979).

——, *The Admission* (produced Almost Free Theatre, London, 1980).

——, *Nixer's Haven* (unperformed).

Norman, Marsha, *Getting Out* (produced Actors Theatre of Louisville, Kentucky, 1977; Lucille Cortel Theatre, New York, 1979) (New York: Dramatists Play Service, 1980).

——, *Third and Oak* (produced Actors Theatre of Louisville, Kentucky, 1978).

——, *Circus Valentine* (produced Actors Theatre of Louisville, Kentucky, 1979).

——, *'night, Mother* (produced The American Repertory Theatre, Boston, 1982; John Golden Theatre, New York, 1983) (New York: Hill and Want, 1983).

——, *The Holdup* (produced New York Circle Repertory Company, New York, 1983; American Conservatory Theatre, San Francisco, 1983).

Bibliography

O'Malley, Mary, *Superscum* (produced Sono Poly, 1972).

——, *A 'Nevolent Society* (produced Open Space, 1974; Theatre Upstairs, 1975).

——, *Oh If Ever a Man Suffered* (produced Soho Poly, 1975; Hampstead Theatre, 1975).

——, *Look Out, Here Comes Trouble* (produced RSC Warehouse, 1978) (Ashover, Derbyshire: Amber Lane Press, 1979).

——, *Once a Catholic* (produced Royal Court, 1977; Wyndham, 1978); in *Best Plays of the 70s*, ed. Stanley Richards (Garden City, New York: Doubleday, 1980).

Owens, Rochelle, *Futz* (produced Minneapolis, 1965; New York, Edinburgh and London, 1967) (New York: Hawk's Well Press, 1961); rev. version in *Futz and What Came After* (1968); in *New Short Plays 2* (London: Methuen, 1969).

——, *The String Game* (produced New York, 1965); in *Futz and What Came After* (1968).

——, *Istanboul* (produced New York, 1965); in *Futz and What Came After* (1968).

——, *Homo* (produced Stockholm and New York, 1966; London, 1969); in *Futz and What Came After* (1968).

——, *Beclch* (produced Theatre of the Living Arts, Philadelphia, and Gate Theatre, New York, 1968); in *Futz and What Came After* (1968).

——, *Futz and What Came After* (includes *Beclch, Homo, The String Game, Istanboul*) (New York: Random House, 1968).

——, *The Karl Marx Play*, music by Galt MacDermot, lyrics by Rochelle Owens (produced American Place Theatre, New York, 1973); in *The Karl Marx Play and Others* (1974).

——, *The Karl Marx Play and Others* (includes *Kontraption, He Wants Shih, Farmer's Almanac, Coconut Folksinger, O.K. Certaldo*) (New York: Dutton, 1974).

——, *He Wants Shih* (produced New York, 1975); in *The Karl Marx Play and Others* (1974).

——, *Emma Instigated Me*, in *Performance Arts Journal I* (produced American Place Theatre, New York, 1976).

——, *The Widow and Me Colonel*, in *Best Short Plays 1977* (New York: Crown Publishers, 1977).

——, *The Queen of Greece*, in *Scenarios* (Yale Theatre, 1980).

——, *Chucky's Hunch* (produced Theatre for the New City, New York).

——, *A Game of Billiards* (unpublished).

——, *Who Do You Want, Peire Vidal?* (produced French Cape Theater).

——, *Three Front* (unpublished).

Page, Louise, *Want-Ad* (1977).

——, *Lucy* (Bristol: Playwrights Co., 1979).

——, *Hearing* (Birmingham Rep., 1979).

——, *Flaws* (produced Sheffield University Drama Studio, 1980).

——, *Angus Del* (produced BBC Radio 4, London, 1980).

——, *House Wives* (produced Derby Playhouse, 1981).

Phillips, Jennifer, *The Backhand Kiss* (produced Phoenix Theatre, Leicester, 1969).

——, *Bodywork* (produced Phoenix Theatre, Leicester, 1972).

——, *Instrument for Love* (produced Almost Free Theatre, London, 1973).

——, *The Antique Baby* (produced Haymarket Theatre, Leicester, 1975).

——, *Daughters of Men* (produced Hampstead Theatre, 1979); radio version published in *Best Radio Plays* (London: Methuen, 1978).

——, *The Canonization of Suzie* (produced Soho Poly Theatre, London, 1980).

Potter, Cherry, *Margie* (produced BBC Radio 3, London, 1975).

——, *Olo* (co-written with Rus Gandy, produced RADA and the Little Theatre, London, 1975).

——, *An Unfairy Tale* (co-written with Caryl Churchill and Mary O'Malley; produced BBC, London, 1975).

——, *Operation Happiness* (*Crown Court* for Granada TV, London, 1976).

——, *Roumanian Roulett* (Thames TV Play, London, 1977).

——, *Seven Little Women*.

——, *Gang-Bang* (*Crown Court* for Granada TV, London, 1979).

——, *Audience or Alice's Hut* (Common Stock Theatre Company, London, 1979).

Sanchez, Sonia, *Sister Son/Ji*, in *New Plays from the Black Theatre* (New York: Bantam Books, 1969).

——, *Uh, Uh, But How Do It Free Us?* (1973).

Schmidman, Jo Ann, *Running Gag* (produced Omaha Magic Theatre, New York, 1979) (Omaha, Nebraska: Omaha Magic Theater Press, 1980).

Shange, Ntozake, *Sassafras* (San Lorenzo, California: Shameless Hussy Press, 1976).

——, *A Photograph: A Study of Cruelty* (produced Public Theatre, New York, 1977).

——, *Where the Mississippi Meets the Amazon* (produced Public Theatre Cabaret, New York, 1977).

——, *Natural Disaster and Other Festive Occasions* (Heirs, 1977).

——, *for colored girls who have considered suicide when the rainbow is enuf* (produced San Francisco, California, 1974) (New York: Macmillan, 1977).

——, *Nappy Edges* (New York: St. Martin's Press, 1978).

——, *Three Pieces* (includes *Spell #7*, *A Photograph: Lovers in Motion*, *Boogie Woogie Landscapes*) (produced New York, 1979) (New York: St. Martin's Press, 1981; Harmondsworth: Penguin Books, 1982).

——, *Mother Courage* (produced New York Shakespeare Theatre, New York).

Terry, Megan, *Beach Grass* (also director: produced Seattle, 1955).

——, *Seascape* (also director: produced Seattle, 1955).

——, *Go Out and Move the Car* (also director: produced Seattle, 1955).

——, *New York Comedy: Two* (also director: produced Seattle, 1955).

——, *The Dirt Boat* (television play, 1955).

——, *Ex-Miss Copper Queen on a Set of Pills* (produced New York, 1965); in *Playwrights for Tomorrow: A Collection of Plays*, vol. 1, ed. Arthur H. Ballet (Minneapolis: University of Minnesota Press, 1966).

——, *When My Girlhood Was Still All Flowers* (produced New York, 1963).

——, *Eat at Joe's* (produced New York, 1964).

——, *Calm Down Mother* (produced New York, 1965; London, 1969) (Indianapolis: Bobbs-Merrill, 1966).

——, *Keep Tightly Closed in a Cool Dry Place* (produced New York, 1965; London, 1968); in *Four Plays* (1967).

——, *The Magic Realists* (produced New York, 1966); in *Three One-Act Plays* (1972).

——, *Comings and Goings* (produced New York, 1966; Edinburgh, 1968); in *Four Plays* (1967).

——, *The Gloaming, Oh My Darling* (produced Minneapolis, 1966); in *Four Plays* (1967).

——, *Viet Rock: A Folk War Movie* (also director: produced New York, 1966); in *Four Plays* (1967).

——, *Four Plays: Viet Rock*; *Comings and Goings*; *Keep Tightly Closed in a Cool Dry Place*; *The Gloaming, Oh My Darling* (New York: Simon & Schuster, 1967).

——, *The Key is on the Bottom* (produced Los Angeles, 1967).

——, *Megan Terry's Home; or, Future Soap* (New York: Samuel French, 1967).

——, *The People vs. Ranchman* (produced Minneapolis, 1967; New York, 1968); with *Ex-Miss Copper Queen on a Set of Pills* (New York: Dramatists Play Service, 1968).

——, *Home* (televised, 1968) (New York: Samuel French, 1972).

——, *Jack-Jack* (produced Minneapolis, 1968).

——, *Massachusetts Trust* (produced Waltham, Massachusetts, 1968); in *The Off-Off-Broadway Book*, ed. Albert Poland and Bruce Mailman (Indianapolis: Bobbs-Merrill, 1972).

——, *Sanibel and Captiva* (broadcast, 1968); in *Three One-Act Plays* (1972).

——, *One More Little Drinkie* (televised, 1969); in *Three One-Act Plays* (1972).

——, *Approaching Simone* (produced Boston and New York, 1970) (Old Westbury, New York: The Feminist Press, 1973).

——, *The Tommy Allen Show* (also director: produced Los Angeles and New York, 1970); in *Scripts 2* (New York), December 1971.

——, *Fireworks* (1970).

——, *Grooving* (produced New York, 1972).

——, *Choose a Spot on the Floor*, with Jo Ann Schmidman (produced Omaha, Nebraska, 1972).

——, *Three One-Act Plays* (includes *Sanibel and Captiva*; *The Magic Realists*; *One More Little Drinkie*) (New York: Samuel French, 1972).

——, *American Wedding Ritual Monitored/Transmitted by the Planet Jupiter* (radio play, broadcast 1972).

——, *Brazil Fado: You're Always with Me* (televised 1972).

——, *Couplings and Groupings* (Theatre Verite) (New York: Pantheon, 1973).

——, *Susan Perutz at the Manhattan Theatre Club* (produced New York, 1973).

——, *Thoughts* (lyrics only), book by Lamar Alford (produced New York, 1973).

210

Bibliography

——, *Nightwalk*, with Sam Shepard and Jean-Claude van Itallie (produced New York, 1973).

——, *St. Hydro Clemency; or, A Funhouse of the Lord: An Energizing Event* (produced New York, 1973).

——, *American Wedding Ritual*, in *Places, A Journal of the Theatre*, vol. 1 (1973).

——, *Hothouse* (produced New York, 1974) (New York: Samuel French, 1975).

——, *All Them Women*, with others (produced New York, 1974).

——, *The Pioneer* (Birmingham, Alabama: Ragnarok Press, 1975).

——, *Willa-Willie Bill's Dope Garden* (Birmingham, Alabama: Ragnarok Press, 1977).

——, *American King's English for Queens* (produced Omaha Magic Theatre, New York, 1978).

——, *100,001 Horror Stories of the Plains* (produced Omaha Magic Theatre, New York, 1978).

——, *Babes in the Bighouse* (produced Omaha Magic Theatre, New York, 1979) (Omaha, Nebraska: Omaha Magic Theatre Press, 1974).

——, *Pro-Game* (produced Omaha Magic Theatre, New York, 1979).

——, *Attempted Rescue on Avenue B* (produced Omaha Magic Theatre, New York, 1979).

——, *Brazil Fado* (produced Omaha Magic Theatre, New York, 1979) (Omaha Nebraska: Omaha Magic Theatre Press, 1980).

——, *Goona-Goona* (produced Omaha Magic Theatre, New York, 1980) (Omaha, Nebraska: Omaha Magic Theatre Press, 1981).

——, *Christmas Copper*.

——, *Kegger* (produced Omaha Magic Theatre, New York, 1982) (Omaha, Nebraska: Omaha Magic Theatre Press, 1983).

Tolan, Kathleen, *A Weekend Near Madison* (produced Louisville Actor's Theater, 1982).

Wandor, Michelene, *The Day After Yesterday* (produced Act Inn Theatre Club, London, 1972).

——, *Spilt Milk* (produced Portable Theatre Workshop, 1973) (published in *Play Nine*, London: Edward Arnold, 1981).

——, *To Die Among Friends* (produced Paradise Foundry, London, 1974); in *Sink Songs* (London: Playbooks, 1976).

——, *Penthesilea* (produced Salt Theatre, London, 1977).

——, *The Old Wives' Tale* (produced Soho Poly, London, 1977).

——, *Care and Control* (produced Gay Sweatshop, London, 1977) (London: Journeyman Press, 1980).

——, *Floorshow* (produced Monstrous Regiment, London, 1977).

——, *Whores D'Oeuvres* (produced Omoro, London, 1978) (London: Hecate, 1980).

——, *Scissors* (produced Almost Free Theatre, London, 1978).

——, *AID Thy Neighbor* (produced Theatre at New End, London, 1978).

——, *Correspondence* (broadcast Radio 4, 'Afternoon Theatre', 1978; produced Institute of Contemporary Arts, London, 1979).

——, *Dust in the Sugar House*, dramatised documentary on writer Antonia White (broadcast Radio 3, 1979).

——, *Aurora Leigh* (produced Mrs Worthington's Daughters, London, 1979); in *Plays by Women*, ed. Michelene Wandor (London: Methuen, 1982).

——, *The Unlit Lamp*, based on the novel by Radclyffe Hall (broadcast Radio 4, 1980).

——, *Precious Bane by Mary Webb* (broadcast Radio 4, London, 1981).

——, *The Ultimate Astonisher* (broadcast Radio 3, London, 1982).

——, *Wild Diamonds* (broadcast Radio 3, London, 1982).

——, *The Ultimate Astonisher* (broadcast Radio 3, London, 1982).

——, *All Out in the Wash* (broadcast BBC TV, London).

——, *Under the Skin* (broadcast BBC TV, London).

Wasserstein, Wendy, *Uncommon Women and Others* (New York: Avon Books, 1978).

Weldon, Fay, *Mixed Doubles: Permanence*; *Words of Advice*; *Friends*; *Mixed Blessings: Second Chance* (produced Orange Tree Theatre, Richmond, 1974).

——, *Moving House* (produced Redgrave Theatre, Farnham, 1976).

——, *Mr. Director* (produced Orange Tree Theatre, Richmond, 1977).

——, *Action Replay* (produced Studio Theatre, Birmingham Repertory, 1978/9; Centrum Theatre, Amsterdam, 1979/80; Orange Tree Theatre, Richmond, 1980).

Bibliography

——, *Polaris* (radio broadcast, London, 1978) (London: Methuen, 1978).

Anthologies that Focus on or Include Substantial Numbers of Feminists Playwrights

France, Rachel (ed.), *A Century of Plays by American Women* (New York: Richards Rosen Press, 1979). This comprises: Megan Terry, *Ex-Miss Copper Queen on a Set of Pills*; Rosalyn Drexler, *Skywriting*; Maria Irene Fornes, *Dr. Kheal*; Clare Boothe Luce, *Slam the Door Softly*; Joan Holden, *The Independent Female*; Karen Malpede, *Lament of Three Women*; Martha Boesing, *Pimp*.

Hoffman, William M. (ed.), *Gay Plays – The First Collection* (New York: Avon Books, 1979). This includes: Susan Miller, *Confessions of a Female Disorder*; Jane Chambers, *A Late Snow*; William Hoffman and Anthony Holland, *Cornbury*.

Moore, Honor (ed.), *The New Women's Theatre – Ten Plays by Contemporary Women* (New York: Vintage Books, 1977). This comprises: Corinne Jacker, *Bits and Pieces*; Tina Howe, *Birth and After Birth*; Honor Moore, *Mourning Pictures*; Myrna Lamb, *I Lost a Pair of Gloves Yesterday*; Eve Merriam, *Out of Our Father's House*; Alice Childress, *Wedding Band*.

Poland, Albert and Bruce Mailman (eds), *The Off-Off-Broadway Book – Plays, People, Theatre* (New York: Bobbs-Merrill, 1972). This comprises: Ruth Krauss, *A Beautiful Day*; Gertrude Stein, *What Happened*; Rosalyn Drexler, *Home Movies*; Tom Eyen, *Why Hanna's Skirt Won't Stay Down*; Rochelle Owens, *Futz*; Megan Terry, *Massachusetts Trust*; Maria Irene Fornes, *Molly's Dream*; Julie Bovasso, *Gloria and Esperanza*; Adrienne Kennedy, *A Rat's Mass*.

Sullivan, Victoria and James Hatch (eds), *Plays By and About Women* (New York: Vintage Books, 1973). This comprises: Lillian Hellman, *The Children's Hour*; Clare Boothe, *The Women*; Megan Terry, *Calm Down Mother*; Maureen Duffy, *Rites*; Alice Childress, *Wine in the Wilderness*.

Richards, Stanley (ed.), *The Best Short Plays* (Radnor, Pennsylvania: Chilton Book Co., 1980). This includes Shirley Lauro, *The Coal Diamond*.

Wandor, Michelene (ed.), *Plays by Women*, vol. 1 (London:

Methuen, 1982). This comprises: Caryl Churchill, *Vinegar Tom*; Pam Gems, *Dusa, Fish, Stas and Vi*; Louise Page, *Tissue*; Michelene Wandor, *Aurora Leigh*.

Wandor, Michelene (ed.), *Strike While the Iron is Hot – Three Plays on Sexual Politics* (London and West Nyack: Journeyman Press, 1980). This comprises: Red Ladder Theatre, *Strike While the Iron is Hot*; Michelene Wandor (Gay Sweatshop), *Care and Control*; Women's Theatre Group, *My Mother Says I Never Should*.

Secondary Sources

Brown, Janet, *Feminist Drama: Definition and Critical Analysis* (Metuchen, New Jersey: Scarecrow Press, 1979).

Chinoy, Helen Krich and Jenkins, Linda Walsh (eds), *Women in American Theater* (New York: Crown Publishers, 1981).

Leavitt, Dinah Luise, *Feminist Theater Groups* (Jefferson, N.C.: McFarland, 1980).

Wandor, Michelene, *Understudies* (London: Eyre Methuen, 1981).

The above brief list includes secondary sources specifically and wholly devoted to feminist drama and theatre or to women in theatre; it does not include general critical or theoretical works on dramas or feminism such as those mentioned at the end of the preface, nor does it include essays or commentaries on feminist drama that appear in journals or other books.

Index

215

Index

Index

Index

Index